yummyPotatoes

yummy Potatoes

65 Downright Delicious Recipes

by **Marlena Spieler**

Photographs by Sheri Giblin

CHRONICLE BOOKS
SAN FRANCISCO

Text copyright © 2007 by Marlena Spieler.
Photographs copyright © 2007 by Sheri Giblin.

Library of Congress Cataloging-in-Publication Data available.

ISBN-10: 0-8118-5646-1
ISBN-13: 978-0-8118-5646-1

Manufactured in China.

Designed by Vivien Sung
Typesetting by Pete Merison
Prop styling by Leigh Noe
Food styling by Dan Becker

Distributed in Canada by Raincoast Books
9050 Shaughnessy Street
Vancouver, British Columbia V6P 6E5

10 9 8 7 6 5 4 3 2 1

Chronicle Books LLC
680 Second Street
San Francisco, California 94107

www.chroniclebooks.com

Acknowledgments

To Alan, whose inner happiness is full of potatoes.

To Dr. Leah Spieler, Jonathan "Potatoes Rock" Harford,
potato-loving Kitty, Gretchen Spieler, Lucy, and the late Big Boy.

To Manuela Barzan and Michele Lomuto, my Nepolitan Chamber
of Commerce buddies who have opened the door to that crazy
delicious place called Naples and its surrounding countryside of
Campania; and to Flavia Vitale, Luca Giordano, and Sonia Carbone,
who have helped us discover, and revel in, all of its tasty goodness;
Soritis Kitrilakis and Rochelle Jolley of Zakynthos, Greece, the
King and Queen of artisanal Greek cheeses from Mount Vikos;
Alexandra Sofis, who has a marvelous appetite, an artistic soul,
and a heart of gold; Katie Goodwin and Jane Milton—the traveling
Spud Queens; the legendary Clark Wolf, who makes good things
happen and is fun to share a pile of New York City french fries with;
Bruce Blackman, for bowls of his deli-delish potato salad, and his
slender wife Etty, who looks as if she has never ever eaten a potato;
the potato man at the Ferry Plaza Farmers' Market, for the most
divine tiny marble potatoes ever; the Old Krakow Polish Restaurant
and Art Café, in San Francisco, for inspiring my passion for potatoes
combined with pickles; Sue Kreitzman, whose book *Potatoes* is as
good an old friend as Sue herself; Trish Kelly, who grew up with an
Irish mother and a kitchen full of potatoes (if you look in Trish's
fridge, you'll always find leftover potatoes, just right for something);
Cary Rudman, who has autographed more books than any author
I know; and Deborah Goldstein, who once looked at me, and apropos
of nothing, exclaimed: "I could do without anything but potatoes!"

To Michael Bauer, Miriam Morgan, and all my wonderful
colleagues at the *San Francisco Chronicle*, which I am enormously
pleased to be part of, each and every time I e-mail a column or drop
in for Thursday lunch.

To my "brother in bacon," Pete Wells, *New York Times*
"Dining In" editor; Nick Fox, deputy "Dining In" editor, for assigning
me fascinating subjects to explore and working with me to get it right;
my potato-loving buddy Kim Severson, *New York Times* writer and
formerly of the *San Francisco Chronicle*, coolest of the cool chicks;

and fellow food lover, *New York Times* writer Julia Moskin, always an inspiration.

To Erik Bruun Bindslev, the International Man of Mystery; HRH Prince Charles, for the organic potatoes I harvested from his garden; Paula Wolfert, for inspiration all the way; Herta Peju of Peju Winery; Bee Wilson; Paul Richardson; Diona Kochilas; Deborah Elliot; Kiwi McLaughlan; Kamala Friedman; Sandy Waks; Carolyn Tillie, Josephine Bacon, Chimicha and Karim Acharki; Steve Sando (also known as Rancho Gordo for his company that grows and sells New World foods, from heirloom beans to pozole); Amanda Hamilton-Hemeter and her love for all things potato; Darrell Corti, wine/sake/olive oil expert, who, hand on heart, says: "I love potatoes as much as anyone could ever love potatoes!"; and Joyce Jue and Wayne Strei, for mashing more garlic-smashed potatoes than seemed humanly possible.

To Zahidul Hakim, the famous NYC cheesemonger, who grew up farming and loving potatoes in Pakistan; to Susie Morgenstern, ("I love potatoes more than anything else in the world"); to June and Cindy, the "angels" of Prince of Wales Close. To the British Potato Council; Jennifer John; chef-owner Roland Passot of La Folie Restaurant in San Francisco, who prepares potatoes elegantly, and his brother Georges Passot, sommelier, who inspiringly pairs them with wine; Catherine Baschet for sharing potatoes in Paris's Le Cordon Bleu kitchen; and to Dr. John and Nichola Fletcher, as well as Thistle the deer, who also truly loves potatoes.

To the French National Potatoes Committee; agronomist and writer Caroline Guinot; chef Charles Soussin; and Alexandre Parmentier of Paris's Le Cordon Bleu ("Yes, I am related to the potato Parmentier").

To Mr. Potato Head for endless childhood joy.

To Edouard Cointreau, Bo Masser, and the World Gourmand Awards, a truly international gathering of food lovers from the far corners of our world, through which I've met many, many wonderful people from all over our planet and come to know so many fascinating places.

To Redzuanan Bih Ismail, known to all in Malaysia as Chef Wan, for sharing with me the wealth of potato dishes I discovered on a recent visit; Mridula Baljekar and David Reay for maken-maken throughout Kuala Lumpur; Mauricio Asta, as always delicious and nutritious; and to friends and fellow potato connoisseurs John Chendo and Esther Novak, and to Esther's late father, Harry Novak, the kugel-king of potatoes.

To Mai Pham of Sacramento's Lemongrass for peaches and pho, though, so far, no potatoes, and her husband, Greg Drescher of the Culinary Institute of America, who organizes splendid international gatherings at the Greystone CIA, where I have been hugely inspired potato-ly; to Athena Vorilla, chic and stylish woman-about-town (the town being Athens, Greece); and to U.K. TV producers Simon and Toby Welfare. To Ted and Roberta Plafker of Beijing, China, and their friends, those potato-loving Russkies Alexey and Anna Nekhzer, who are convinced that the best potatoes in the world come from Irkutsk, Siberia.

To Peru—thank you for the potatoes; and to James Shenk and his restaurant, Destino, for his passion for all goodies Peruvian; as well as fellow Peruvian Dr. Noah Stroe, who always has a potato recipe to offer when I mention his childhood home country; to Sara Beatriz Guardia of Lima.

Bill LeBlond and Amy Treadwell: Once again, it's been great fun . . . and this time, fun with potatoes!

With grateful thanks to Mark Phillip Mawson and his Tara, beautiful in every way.

Thank you, Madeleine, best friend and wonderful cat that you are.

Table of Contents

Table of Contents

Introduction

Potatoes are wonderful

Hearty and sustaining, they are full of potassium and vitamin C, rich with A, B_1, and B_6, with a nice dose of iron and fiber, too. They have only 90 calories on their own and are bereft of any fat—though we all know how alluring a big pat of butter is, when it comes to spuds.

On average, Americans eat 142.7 pounds of potatoes each year. In Ireland, and some other parts of Europe, the average annual consumption is over 200 pounds per head. The Irish, and Scottish, are justifiably proud of their potato-eating ways. With their renowned sweet tooth, the Scots even use potatoes to make a chocolate marzipan-like sweet: simply knead a little mashed potato with lots of confectioners' sugar and cocoa. But Eastern Europe, too, is a potato-eating land. Without potatoes, goulash would just be soup. Without potatoes, Russian pot roasts would just be meat and gravy. And once, in a German market, I thought a potato festival was in progress, as every member of the community seemed to be gathered together in the throes of potato eating. There were big mounds of potatoes, fried with onions; great griddles of sizzling potato pancakes; vats of mustardy potato salad. But no, it was not a special occurrence; this potato festival was simply the weekly marketplace among the potato-loving townsfolk.

Potatoes are able to parlay even the most meager of ingredients into an always-satisfying, often-inspiring meal. Cook them with onions and you transform the most humble of ingredients into Potatoes Lyonnaise. Make a potato soup with an onion or leek and you have a creamy, homey soup that is a meal. Artist Paul Cézanne's favorite dish was boiled potatoes sprinkled with extra-virgin olive oil and chopped onion. In Peru, one might eat a bowl of earthy lavender-fleshed potatoes, sprinkled with salt, hot pepper sauce, and lime juice. When I lived on the island of Crete, I ate the local *taverna*-prepared potatoes roasted in hot embers, split open, and sprinkled with a dash of wine vinegar and a handful of baby greens, perhaps peas, from the garden or the fields. Such simplicity is delicious.

Or you can lavish your potatoes with great indulgence—fluff them with cream and truffles, roast them toasty brown and splash with extra-virgin olive oil, slather them with aioli, or layer slices with mountain cheeses.

Almost everyone loves potatoes, during good times and bad. Potatoes enhance, they soothe. They are like—well—potatoes are like comfort in a sack. According to a Southwest Airlines *Spirit* magazine survey, mashed potatoes ranks in the top five of America's comfort foods. But I didn't need a survey to tell me that, and you probably don't either; what soothes better than one of a zillion dishes prepared with potatoes? Even just a plain potato, sometimes *especially* just a plain potato! Eat it in a bowl with a spoon, with slippers on your feet and your devoted cat or pup at your lap, looking longingly toward your spuds.

Potatoes can also be a very neat little weapon in the arsenal of love; in fact, they just might be the way to snap up the object of your affections, captivating your beloved forevermore. After all, who can resist a lover who possesses a magician's way with potatoes? Could you *really* leave someone who makes the perfect garlic mash? Or crusty gratin?

Almost all nationalities eat potatoes. While I expect to find potatoes in Europe, it is in Asia that I'm amazed at how very popular our spud is—in India, Pakistan, Bangladesh, and, surprisingly, Malaysia, potatoes fill out the savory spicy stews and coconutty curries. In Mexico, potatoes are right at home with local chiles. The Vietnamese love their french fries, and I've eaten crunchy Indonesian fries topped with spicy chile-garlic paste. Yummmmmm. Greeks and Turks serve potatoes in the most savory, cozy long-simmered treats, and even Japan has embraced the potato. I've found "steaks of potato" topped with miso and sesame seeds, creamy potatoes mashed with wasabi, as well as the potato croquette that is ubiquitous in modern, casual Japanese restaurants.

Babies like potatoes cooked until very tender, cut into chunks to grab in chubby fists, or mashed with milk and butter. For some of us, the baby within never goes away; is anything really better than mashed potatoes? Earthy potato flavor, a cloud of creamy, smooth potato fluff—eat it by itself in a bowl, as a side dish with meat loaf or roasted chicken, or with crisp-skinned sausages for the British classic Bangers and Mash.

And all socioeconomic classes eat potatoes. Peasants eat potatoes. University professors eat potatoes. Teachers, doctors, street sweepers—most eat, and love, potatoes. Great chefs serve potatoes to their well-heeled customers. Diner cooks sling potato hash on their griddles, and fast-food cooks plunge french fries into hot oil with regularity.

Restaurants serve butter-browned potatoes next to the steak or tiny boiled potatoes next to the trout; school cafeterias scoop up a snowy mound of mash alongside the Salisbury steak; bars serve potatoes in savory, snacky ways, such as potato skins; tapas bars serve Potatoes Riojana; and people make potatoes in an unending variety of ways at home.

Having a bowl of boiled potatoes in the fridge is a boon for busy adults—a pot can be cooked on Sunday and get you through a good part of the week's menus: end-of-the-day salads; comforting home fries and hash browns; crisp little roesti, sliced, browned, and sprinkled with a persillade to accompany a steak, or sliced up into a warm salad of frisée and bacon.

Baked potatoes are delicious, especially if you are a kid or a senior, and find mealtime challenging. Pop the scrubbed potato into a medium-hot oven and leave it alone. When it has roasted, after about an hour, its skin is crunchy and darkly flavorful, its insides tender potato goodness, ready to slather with butter, drown with a spoonful of sour cream, and shower with chives. And, for the lavish among us, might I mention that caviar is a classic addition to baked potato and sour cream, and anything truffly was just meant to be melted into a baked potato; also, if I may continue in this direction, a sliver of foie gras melts decadently into a fire-roasted potato. For healthful simplicity, however, nothing beats a spoonful of yogurt, some chopped onions, and perhaps a sprinkling of paprika and cumin over the top.

Gratins and scalloped potatoes are irresistible, and I defy anyone, regardless of age, to just say "No." Personally, I could not possibly pass up a casserole filled with the crispy browned edges and the creamy soft potato layers within, oozing cheese and cream, and sometimes permeated with the aroma of shallots, onions, and ham.

Then there are french fries—*frites,* chips, whatever you call them. These sticks of potato fried in hot oil until golden and tender have captured culinary adoration in nearly every land on this planet. Would a hamburger be complete without them? Britain's national dish, fish and chips, would simply be fried fish without the "chips," Brit-speak for big fat french fries. (While fish might need chips, chips don't need fish; consider the "chip butty," a northern delicacy of white bread, chips, and tangy brown sauce.) Greeks fry potatoes in olive oil, then sprinkle them with salt mixed with crushed oregano. Tunisians make olive oil potatoes and eat them with a hot chile and spice sauce. Israelis tuck them into a pita along with falafel, vegetable garnish, and varied sauces. The Vietnamese are known to toss french fries into a stir-fry, and Bulgarians add them to a meaty stew, while Canadians pile them up and drench them in a meaty wine sauce and a handful of cheesy curds and call it *poutine.*

Basically, though, it's all potato: a delicious tuber, member of the nightshade family, whose starchy flesh can be cooked hundreds, probably thousands, of ways.

Anyone can have a kitchen stocked with potatoes; they are sold in any grocery. Simply buy a bag when you think of it; they wait on the shelf patiently until you're ready to cook them up. If you are ambitious, plant a little potato patch—you'll be rewarded with potatoes that are so aromatic, fresh, and delicious, you'll find your feeling toward potatoes utterly amplified.

And as enthusiastic as I might be about potatoes, there are others who surpass even me—my husband, for instance. When I mused about writing a book devoted to potatoes, he went out and bought the biggest bag he could, as encouragement. "My Celtic heart skipped a happy little beat when I heard you mention the possibility of a potato book. I thought about all the recipe tasting."

Note: For those who miss sweet potatoes and wonder where they are; the sweet-fleshed tubers and their yammy relatives are not potatoes at all.

There is simply not enough space between these covers to do delicious justice to both potatoes and the sweet ones!

A Pile of Potatoes

Once, years ago, I was invited by friends to stay at their Dutch countryside farmhouse while they went away. "The place is empty," they said, "use it and enjoy."

My husband and I arrived without provisions, hungry, not knowing that it was the start of a holiday weekend, and banks, shops, and restaurants were all closed for the next four days.

We found the keys, let ourselves in, then tried to figure out what to eat. As the shops were closed and our money unusable until we exchanged it, we foraged around the farmhouse kitchen. There were a few onions, some oil, a handful of herbs and spices—ingredients to cook with, but nothing to assuage our hunger. Nothing to make a meal.

As our stomachs growled, and as evening drew, we looked out the window to survey our surroundings. There, across the road, I saw a mountain, or a pile the size of a mountain, of potatoes next to a farmhouse, and no one was home. Everyone in this country seemed to be on vacation.

So—waiting for the cover of darkness—I picked up a few potatoes from the mountain, tucked them into my pockets, and took them home. We ate potato soup, and it was delicious. We slept cozy and well-fed.

The next morning, I thought, a few more potatoes, breakfast potatoes, I can fry them in a pan! I gathered a handful in the folds of my skirt and returned to our kitchen.

We ate the best pan-fried potatoes, enhanced with a handful of sliced onions. I decided on a potato omelet for dinner—I had already met a few pecking chickens on my forays into potato stealing, and as I was living the life of a thief, I followed a chicken and was deliciously rewarded.

And so it went for days, until the holiday was over, the neighbors came back home, the shops opened, and we headed out of town.

I never confessed my thieving ways. I was simply too cowardly.

I did notice, though, that with a pile of potatoes, you'll never go hungry. And you'll never really get bored because there are simply so many delicious things to do with them. You don't need to steal them. You can just buy a big bag—they range from affordable to downright cheap. It's one of the potato's most endearing qualities. Okay, some potatoes are exotic and pricey, and suitably wonderful and exciting, but there is almost always a potato for your budget, as well as your tastes.

And once you've purchased your big bag of potatoes, you have a meal for almost any time of the day—breakfast, lunch, dinner, or midnight snack—and for almost every emotional feeling and desire.

Potato History

From high in the Andes to the streets of Paris, the fields of Ireland, and the steppes of Eastern Europe, potatoes have flourished and nourished whole cultures whose diets are based on them. Potatoes are now grown in more than eighty countries. There are over a thousand named varieties, about seven hundred in major seed banks or libraries, and many others without names at all, though, sadly, for commercial cultivation there are only about one hundred types.

Potatoes are native to the highlands of Peru in South America and were enjoyed by the Inca peoples in the Andes mountains at least eight thousand years ago. From tiny nut-size morsels to something quite like our own baking potatoes of today, the Incas not only ate a wide variety of potatoes as their staple food but cultivated varieties in myriad colors, shapes, and textures. The potato was everyday nourishment, yet was also regarded as having spiritual qualities.

It is believed that the Spanish conquistadors discovered potatoes around 1537. Some of the earliest European writings about these knobby tubers date from about 1550, and they were introduced to Great Britain about forty years later. Though Sir Walter Raleigh and Sir Francis Drake often get credit for toting them to Britain from Virginia—the potato apparently having arrived in Virginia via Spanish traders who had obtained it from the Incas—it most likely was a nameless Spanish sailor who brought samples of potatoes from the Andes back to his home in Spain. And from there, they worked their way up to England.

The potato was not initially embraced as a food in Western Europe, though. As a member of the nightshade family, its leaves are poisonous, and people were afraid of the tubers, too. But life was changing and people were hungry; both social and agricultural changes combined to convince people of the potato's inherent goodness. Ireland was the first country to embrace the miracle vegetable. (Alas, as the people of Ireland flourished on the mysterious tuber, so too did they suffer famine when the crops were destroyed by blight, driving a huge migration of Irish to look for a new life in America.)

It was the late sixteenth century when the potato arrived in France. Everyone admired its beauty—Marie Antoinette wore potato flowers in her hair and gardeners planted potatoes everywhere, for their beautiful blooms and foliage—but people were too frightened to eat any part of the plant. You could say they were phobic, no doubt based on the nightshade family connection. Experts linked the potato to a variety of ailments from leprosy to syphilis, from rickets to uncontrollable flatulence. It took a long, long time and a great deal of convincing before it was realized that the tuber, or root of the potato, was safe (and delicious) to eat.

Antoine-Auguste Parmentier was an army pharmacist who had survived on the starchy tuber as a prisoner of the Seven Years' War in Westphalia. From this experience, he knew that potatoes were edible and sustaining. When the famine of 1770 was wreaking starvation, he decided to convince the population that the potato was not only safe to eat, but it was also a food that could nourish the starving people of France. Louis XVI granted Parmentier the land on which to grow an experimental crop, then Parmentier served his harvest at an all-potato banquet for the royal court, held at the Hôtel des Invalides. From potato soup to potato salad, potato fritters, and potato bread, ending with potato liqueur—I think there were eleven courses in all—the royals were delighted, and eventually so was all of France. Today, in France, the term "Parmentier" is used for any dish that contains potatoes, and there is a street in Paris, as well as a metro stop, that bears the name.

In the early nineteenth century, Greece also had a difficult time convincing the people that the potato was a good thing to eat. The first president of modern Greece, Kapodistrias, had tasted potatoes when he was a diplomat in Russia or on one of his many other European travels. Like Parmentier, he knew the goodness that the potato had to offer the hungry peasants and had a huge shipment of potatoes delivered to the docks of Piraeus. But when he tried to give them away, the peasants were suspicious and ignored both him and his strange tubers. Kapodistrias, however, knew his fellow Greeks well. He had the mountain of potatoes surrounded by a fence and posted guards to watch over them around the clock. Within the week, all of the potatoes had disappeared. Potatoes have been a delicious favorite of the Greeks ever since—and *soooo* delicious, as anyone who has ever forked up a mouthful of lemon potatoes can tell you.

North America got off no more easily. Despite its being a New World food, the potato made its way to the North American table via an influx of Scotch-Irish immigrants who brought the tuber to Londonderry, New Hampshire, in 1719. By midcentury, however, many New Englanders were still convinced that eating potatoes could shorten one's life. Now, of course, could you imagine chowder without potatoes, or New England boiled dinner sans spuds?

In the British Isles, it wasn't until the late eighteenth century that potatoes became a staple. The backdrop to their arrival was the change from a feudal society, the increased demands of towns, and disastrous grain harvests. Potatoes were easier to grow than grains, more tolerant of cold and wet weather, and exempt from the grain tax laws. Soon the spud was crowned the food of the poor.

For those who really love potatoes, you may wish to be in touch with CIP, the Centro Instituto de Papas (the International Potato Center), located in La Molina, Peru, near Lima. The institute houses a library and research station devoted to improving sustainable cultivation, preserving and reintroducing disappeared varieties, and supporting research—via potatoes—toward a world with less poverty, more health, and a better environment. A focus for diplomatic personnel, dignitaries, and international visitors, the CIP has a guest house and other facilities for gatherings.

And a note in the modern history of the amazing potato: In 1995 a potato plant was taken into space on board the shuttle *Columbia*, to be cultivated there, making the potato the first food to be grown in space!

About the Potato

The Latin name for the potato plant is *Solanum tuberosum*, which indicates that it is part of the *Solanaceae*, or nightshade, botanical family. This family includes tomatoes, eggplants, and peppers, as well as deadly nightshade. In fact, every part of the plant, apart from the tubers, is mildly poisonous and should not be eaten. Hence the one-time fear of Europeans about eating the potato (as well as eggplants and tomatoes).

Choose potatoes that are the freshest, most unblemished looking. Avoid any that are cracked, bruised, soft, wrinkled, or spotted with green. (If your stored potatoes turn green, cut off all the green portions; if they are very green, discard the whole potato.) When your potatoes are being stored, check up on them every so often. If you find any sprouting taters, bury them in a pot of dirt, pat down, and water gently. Place outside in the sun, and water every day. Shoots will spring from the earth and grow into a plant; when flowers have started to blossom, pull up the plant and dig up the five or six little potatoes resting at its roots. You will be rewarded by the tastiest, nuttiest, earthiest little morsels; few things are more delicious than freshly dug baby potatoes.

Floury potatoes store well; new waxy potatoes do not. In the right conditions, potatoes should last about two weeks; for young potatoes, plan on eating them within a few days of purchase. The exception for eating the freshest potatoes possible is the Italian potato dumpling, gnocchi. They must be made using old potatoes, stored from last year's harvest.

When storing, potatoes should be kept in a dark, dry, coolish (45°F to 50°F) place, unwashed. If they are stored in the light, they turn green and should not be eaten because of possible varying toxicity, as noted previously. Storing potatoes in too warm a place makes them sprout, soften, and wrinkle. Storing them in too cold a place, such as the refrigerator, tends to turn the starches to sugar and develop an unwelcome sweetness. Also, when stored for extended periods, or if harvested late in the season, the sugar content of the potatoes increases. Too high a sugar content interferes with the potatoes' hearty, savory earthiness and causes them to brown too fast—before they cook through or crisp up—if they are destined for the fryer.

And potatoes do *not* freeze well. If your potatoes are in danger of deteriorating and sprouting, plant them. One of the prized features of potatoes is the fact that you can keep them around for weeks and they will be ready at any time to boil, mash, bake, or fry your way to happiness. Storing works best for baking potatoes. New potatoes are just that: young, tender, fresh. The difference between freshly dug potatoes and those that have been around for a little while is huge, the same difference between out-of-season cold-storage tomatoes and sun-warmed ones straight from the garden.

All potatoes are good, but tasting your way through a wide variety and being a bit picky about your potatoes can only enhance your spud-munching experience. But take a bite; you should taste bland starch, rich texture, and, above all, a whiff of earth, a taste of fresh damp dirt.

With the hundreds of—no, make that over a thousand—potato varieties available, it's too hard to list all of them. Basically, potatoes fall into three main categories: floury, waxy, and a medium waxy-floury category, called all-purpose, somewhere in between. Potatoes' qualities are determined by the amount of moisture and starch in them. These are what make potatoes floury, waxy, creamy, or dry.

The potato's flavor—like that of other fruits and vegetables—depends upon the terroir: the particular soil, climate, moisture, length of the seasons, and daylight hours. Like other vegetables and fruits, a good potato will taste of the land it is grown in. A mediocre potato will taste of very little and will mostly just give a starchy hit.

Long before I learned about terroir, I had my own potato epiphany: I dug up tiny new potatoes from just under the soil and cooked them for only a few minutes until tender. They tasted so delicate, so earthy and flavorful, with only a slick of butter melting on top and a green onion munched alongside. The soil, the rainfall, the temperature of the season, had all contributed; I thought I could even taste the personality of the person who had planted the spuds. After that, I paid attention to the farmers' markets for my potato needs and kept an eye open for particularly good spuds.

Look for specific varieties when you buy potatoes, as each potato has different qualities. Ask the farmers at the farmers' market about their potatoes and which are best for your favorite dishes and recipes. Be wary of all-purpose pota-toes, as they can be good for almost any potato recipe, but not sensational on their own.

Smaller potatoes with a thinner skin are young, new, and waxy, with moist flesh; they tend to keep their shape when cooked. The starch that gives these potatoes their characteristic waxy quality is called amylopectin, much like the pectin in fruits that holds jams and jellies together. Fingerlings, creamers, Pink Fir Apple, La Ratte—all are delicious young potatoes, with a pleasant, almost chewy texture. Young potatoes have a thin skin that you can scrub or rub away; if the potatoes are truly young, the skin will just fall away. Potatoes like this really excel in salad. New potatoes can be really, really tiny; called culls, or marbles, they are tiny little morsels of fresh, fresh potato flavor. If you are at a farmers' market and happen to find these tiny potatoes, treat yourself to a delightful dish: roast them with a little olive oil and rosemary, or boil them quickly.

Larger potatoes are older, with a lower moisture content, and therefore more floury. Often, the same variety of potato can be either waxy or floury depending on its age. Floury potatoes will cook up fluffy, bake up deliciously dry to burst out of a baked potato, and fall apart into soft airy puffs; this is due to their particular starch, known as amylose. Amylose makes gnocchi particularly light and puréed soups nice and creamy, though if boiled, floury potatoes tend to fall apart, especially if cooked that little bit too long. The most classic, tasty baking potato is a russet, but don't think when you walk into a supermarket that if it looks like a russet it will have that same earthy flavor; sometimes supermarkets sell less tasty, more easily and quickly grown potatoes, practical for business purposes but simply not as richly potatoey tasting as the russet.

Heirloom and lesser-known breeds of potatoes, like Yukon Gold or Maya Gold, are juicy and succulent and good for almost any purpose, depending on their size and age. Truly all-purpose, keeping their shape when boiled, the golden flesh also yields a delicious flavor and sunny color. In Malaysia, I ate tiny, knobby, utterly delicious potatoes, simmered in a soy-spiked savory sauce or a coconutty curry, and in Greece the local potatoes have a white-yellow flesh, very tasty for nearly all purposes. Blue potatoes have a deep purple-blue flesh, and a minerally, earthy flavor. To keep the color in, boil with their skins on and don't overcook; the flesh will be shockingly, delightfully, indigo-lavender. Red-fleshed potatoes are found in the United States and also grown in Scotland; an heirloom, or revived, breed, they taste delicious.

Older potatoes have a thicker skin, as the thickness increases with age of harvest and length of storage. The potato skin is sometimes considered the most delicious part; however, if the potatoes are very old and the skins tough, or if you want to cook a dish of refined potato flesh rather than earthy skin, simply peel them. Some object to peeling potatoes because the skin is significantly higher in fiber and minerals than the flesh. Though this is true, it is such a thin area that the overall amount is insignificant. I recommend that the decision to peel or not to peel is according to your own taste and patience with a potato peeler. If the potato is young, don't bother to peel. If it is an older potato that promises a thick, rough skin, peel then throw either away or toss the skins with a little olive oil and coarse salt, and roast until crispy, crunchy, golden brown.

Potato Products

Dried potatoes from Peru are mountain-dried potato chunks, used by the indigenous people in the Andes. Often, the dried potatoes will be added to a soup, sometimes one that contains several other types of potatoes, one for a floury texture and one waxy, in addition to the chewier mountain-dried ones.

Potato starch is much like cornstarch or arrowroot, at its best for crisp fried batters, or a small amount added to a cake of ground nuts or a torte.

Dehydrated mashed potato flakes may be found in institutional eating halls, dismayingly plain and pasty, but actually, they are not bad at all for making gnocchi as their utter dryness can result in light, light gnocchi.

Frozen—yep. I've seen 'em. But I'm going to pretend I haven't. Unless it's an emergency and you must have potatoes or you will die. Then you can use frozen.

Potato chips. No explanations needed. We all know these naughty, delicious things.

Potato milk is a new nondairy product for the lactose-intolerant. I've heard it's not bad in coffee.

Fats That Potatoes Love

Okay, we know that potatoes are not fattening and that, on their own, you have only 90 calories of fat-free nutrition and delight. However, the truth is also that potatoes *loooove* fats. They become luxurious, rich, seductive, and irresistible with fats. Here are some of the fats that potatoes love.

Bacon fat: Don't tell anyone, but slipping a spoonful or two into homemade hash browns or home fries makes them very tasty.

Butter: *Aaaaah.* Potatoes and butter. Melted butter on a baked potato, or a boiled one. Little sliced potatoes sautéed in butter. A buttery gratin. Does life get any better than this? And don't even *think* of margarine. Just don't.

Duck, goose, or chicken fat: The rich fat from poultry is *soooo* yummy with potatoes, conjuring up the flavors of eastern Europe—drizzled over boiled potatoes, mashed with potatoes and onions for a filling for pierogi or ravioli, tossed with potatoes for roasting. Purchase duck or goose fat in a jar, or render your own fat by placing bits and pieces of duck, goose, or chicken in a skillet with a chopped onion and water to cover. Bring to a simmer, cover, and cook until the fat renders out of the meat. Remove from the heat, cool, and chill; skim the fat off the top and use as desired. If you're roasting duck, goose, or chicken, spoon off the fat and drippings as the poultry roasts and save it for your roasting or other potato needs.

Lard and beef suet: Used for frying chips, *frites,* and french fries. It is said that french fries are at their best when cooked in horse fat; traditional English chippies are fried in beef suet or lard. When you're eating crisp fries of any kind, there is nothing better than animal fat—with the exception of olive oil, which makes divine fries. Bland vegetable oils just don't give the true, rich potato flavor and texture.

Olive oil: There is little that's better with potatoes than olive oil, and olive oil is very healthful, too, so you can bask in both deliciousness and well-being. Use extra-virgin for flavor or for stewing and braising, pure or virgin olive oil for frying.

Vegetable oils: Bland oils are okay for some crisp frying such as potato pancakes. Use when you want a crisp edge but no flavor.

Break

I'm a breakfast person. I love my cup of coffee on a weekday, perhaps sourdough toast topped with goat cheese and a handful of herbs plopped down on it, maybe a bowl of oatmeal. But on weekends, breakfast means a big meal, one that might work its way into lunch, or even dinner. When we were children, Sunday breakfast meant a meal like that, seeming to span the day, with a stream of family and friends stopping by to join in.

A weekend breakfast can mean only one thing: potatoes! From hash browns to hash, from home fries to potato cakes to stovies, breakfast potatoes need a bit of a crisp crust, a creamy interior, a contrast of earthy, soft, and crunchy, a kaleidoscope of potato flavors and textures. Breakfast potatoes are divine. They can get you out of bed on the weekend, and get you through the week's drudgery just thinking about them.

Omelets or huevos rancheros, a pile of silky smoked salmon or poached eggs, sizzlingly juicy sausages, and crisp crunchy bacon—breakfast is always better with a mound of crunchy potatoes.

fast
Potatoes

The Best
Hash Browns/Home Fries

○ ● ○ ◐ ○ ●

The secret to great hash browns or superb home fries is having good precooked potatoes, potatoes that have been cooked long enough to stabilize their starch but not so long as to go mushy. It is generally—but not always—accepted that hash browns are made from shredded or finely diced potatoes (and often made into a crisp cake), whereas home fries are of the chunky variety, a pile of crispy, crunchy browned potato morsels. Both are yummy, and although they are different in the end result, they start out the same: boiled potatoes headed for a skillet. Frankly, I think one of the mistakes people make is adding too many ingredients. Remember, it's all about the potatoes. A few goodies here and there can perk up the plate, but too many extra ingredients can interfere with the lusciously potato flavor.

◇ Serves 4

8 medium waxy potatoes, about 1½ lbs total, whole and unpeeled (you can use potatoes that you have boiled up to a week ahead of time)

Salt

4 to 6 tablespoons butter, or a combination of butter and olive oil, as needed

Freshly ground black pepper

1 to 2 tablespoons chopped fresh chives, garlic, parsley, or thinly sliced green onions (optional)

1 Place the potatoes in a saucepan with salted water to cover. Bring to a boil, reduce the heat to medium-high, and cook until the potatoes are half cooked through; that is, your knife or fork can permeate them a bit, but then it gets crunchy. Remove the potatoes from the heat and drain; cool until you can handle them. If you have a stash of already–cooked potatoes, you're halfway to your hash browns or home fries; you can omit this boiling step. Day- or two-day-old boiled potatoes work even better than freshly cooked ones.

2 For hash browns: Shred the potatoes over the large holes of a box grater or food processor; do not bother to peel, as the peel will mostly come off as you shred them. Whatever bits of skin remain, you can pick them out or leave them in. They tend to disappear in the crispness of the potatoes.

For home fries: Simply cut the potatoes up into somewhat uneven chunks or thick slices. Again, to peel or not to peel is your own decision, according to your own taste.

3 Heat a heavy, large nonstick skillet, and add about half the butter.

4 For hash browns: Add the shredded potatoes to the hot pan in a thick layer, pressing down with the spatula for even browning. Cook over medium heat, raising or lowering the heat so that you get an even browning as they cook. Turn the potatoes over every so often, in thick chunks, so that you get crisp-edged outsides and creamy, tender potato insides. You don't need it to be completely a pancake, only a mixture of pancake and hash textures.

For home fries: Add the cut-up potatoes to the hot pan, over medium to medium-high heat, letting them brown nicely on one side before turning them over, then after five to ten minutes, turning them again. As you turn them each time, they will break into differently sized pieces and develop a selection of textures of tenderness, with crisp edges.

5 Season to taste with salt and pepper, then serve hot, sprinkled with your herb of choice, alongside whatever eggs you choose. This is one time that I might just say, "Reach for the ketchup."

Variations:

Bratkartoffeln
(A savory German potato-fest)

Spoon several tablespoons of beef broth or defatted meat juices, from some delicious leftover that you've been saving for just this reason, into the pan with the browning potatoes and onions, and sprinkle with salt and pepper to taste. The potatoes and onions will get soft for a minute or two; continue cooking, raising the heat if you need to, and cook for a few minutes until the potatoes and onions crisp up again. They are done when they are a browned, tangled, very savory mess. Serve hot and crispy, sprinkled with 1 to 2 tablespoons chopped fresh parsley. You can make these with duck or goose fat, chicken fat, or bacon fat added to the olive oil, yes you can!

Gretchen's House Potatoes
also known as Onion Turbo-Charged Potatoes

Parboil 1 pound heirloom potatoes as directed in step 1, then drain and cool. Cut into thick slices or chunks and brown as directed, with the inclusion of 1 to 2 chopped or sliced onions—I like a combination of both chopped and sliced, for a variety of textures when the onions cook up. Cook over medium heat, letting the potatoes and onions brown, turning them with your spatula only enough to keep them browning evenly—you don't want them to brown too darkly; rather, you want them to turn golden. The onions will go limp as the potatoes brown, and start browning themselves.

Duskie Estes' Spud-a-Rama

Duskie, the adorable co-owner and chef of Sonoma's Zazu and Bovolo, just *loooooves* a spud-a-rama, adapted from her teenage haunt, San Francisco's late, great Spaghetti Western dive/restaurant. Pile fresh home fries onto a plate, then top with masses of shredded sharp Cheddar. Pop in the oven for a few minutes to melt. Serve sprinkled with tons of thinly sliced green onions and diced tomatoes, with a fried egg right on top. To quote Duskie: "Dude, it's so good!"

Huevos Estilo Andalucía

Eggs Poached in Potato-Pepper-Tomato Sauce

○ ● ○ ● ○ ●

Potatoes, slowly cooked into a vibrant hash with peppers and tomatoes, a poached
egg or two nestling into the savory saucy mixture. Pure soul of Andalucía.
Eat for breakfast, supper, or as a middle-of-the-night snack, with a slice or two
of excellent *jamon serrano* or salami alongside, if you wish.

◇ Serves 2
(allowing 2 eggs per person), or 4 (with 1 egg per person)

3 to 4 tablespoons extra-virgin olive oil, or as needed

1 big onion, cut into 1/2-inch dice

**2 to 3 big baking potatoes, peeled and cut into
1/2- to 3/4-inch dice**

1/2 red bell pepper, cut into 1/2-inch dice

1/2 green bell pepper, cut into 1/2-inch dice

**3 to 4 big, fat raw tomatoes, diced (if it's winter, use
canned tomatoes, plus some of their canning juice)**

Salt

4 small garlic cloves or 3 fat ones, chopped

Red pepper flakes, or freshly ground black pepper

Large pinch of cumin

2 or 4 eggs

**2 to 3 tablespoons chopped fresh flat-leaf parsley
or cilantro**

1 In a large, nonstick heavy skillet, heat the olive oil over
medium-high heat, and lightly brown the onion with the potatoes, turning until they are golden and just tender; add the red
and green bell peppers and cook for a further 5 or so minutes.

2 Add the tomatoes. Sprinkle with salt to taste and cook for a
few more minutes, turning once or twice, to cook the tomatoes
until no longer raw but not too saucy. They should still be like
tomatoes, not like sauce.

3 Toss in the garlic, red pepper flakes, and cumin, season to
taste with salt, and make indentations for either 2 or 4 eggs.
Break an egg into each indentation and cover. Cook over
medium-low heat until the whites have firmed up but the yolks
are still runny.

4 Serve sprinkled with the parsley, and eat right away.

Variation

A Meaty Alternative:

**Add six to eight ounces sliced chorizo (for a Mexican flavor)
or merguez (for deliciously Moroccan or Tunisian taste) to the
onions and potatoes. If the potato mixture is too oily, pour off
some of the excess fat as it cooks out of the sausages.**

Papeta pur Eeda

Parsee Potatoes with Cumin, Chile, and Poached Egg

○ ● ○ ◑ ○ ●

"We Parsees love our eggs!" exclaimed Cyrus Todiwala, of London's Café Spice Namaste. "We do . . . and we also love our potatoes. We could not live without potatoes!" Cyrus was showing me one of his favorite dishes, potatoes cooked in a pan and topped with eggs. It had lots of cumin, my favorite spice, and a ton of cilantro—I added more, of course—and it smelled promising as I watched him add the potatoes to the pan, then crack the eggs on top.

"See that woman over there, she could not live without potatoes!" Cyrus was in full-flow, enthusiasm-wise; "that woman over there" was, in fact, his wife and the co-owner of Café Spice Namaste. This is my adapted version of the dish he made for us that day and one that continues to evolve in my kitchen. It's potato-filling and hearty, but the spice lifts it from its winter sphere and makes it bright and zesty.

◇ Serves 4

2 to 3 tablespoons vegetable oil, or a combination of oil and butter (I often use olive oil, a trend among chic modern Indians, too)

1 teaspoon cumin seeds

2 very large baking potatoes, 2 or 3 medium ones, or 4 small to medium ones, peeled and sliced 1/8-inch thick, then blanched

1 onion, cut crosswise or lengthwise into thin slices

1/2 to 1 mildish green chile, chopped

2 to 3 garlic cloves, coarsely chopped

Salt

3 to 5 tablespoons chopped cilantro

Pepper

4 eggs

Large pinch of ground cumin

Fresh homemade chutney (facing page), or hot sauce

1 In a large, nonstick heavy skillet, heat a tablespoon or so of the oil over medium-high heat, then add the cumin seeds and sizzle them in the hot oil for a few seconds. Push to one side and add the potatoes and onion, letting them cook for a few minutes until a bit softened, then add the chile, garlic, and remaining oil. Cook for about 4 minutes, tossing once or twice, then season with salt.

2 Add salted water to just below the top of the potatoes, cover the pan, and cook on low heat until the potatoes are just tender but firm enough not to get mushy, for 5 to 10 minutes.

3 Sprinkle in half the cilantro, turn the potatoes around in it, and season to taste with salt and pepper. Then, using an egg, make indentations in four locations where you will then open each egg and plop it right in. If you are very hungry, have two eggs.

4 Cover the pan and let the eggs cook in the steam of the simmering potatoes. Cook until the whites are opaque and firmish and the yolks are still soft but perhaps very lightly veiled.

5 Sprinkle with the ground cumin and the rest of the cilantro, and cut into four portions, each one with an egg. Serve with fresh chutney.

Fresh Chutney

Put 3 garlic cloves in a food processor and add a nugget of fresh ginger, then whirl together with half of or a whole fresh green chile pepper, chopped. When this is puréed, add 1/2 cup cilantro and 1/2 cup fresh mint or parsley. Add the juice of half a lemon or lime, about 1/2 teaspoon cumin, and salt to taste. I could eat this by the spoonful—and I have.

Car Breakdown on a Greek Island, Mechanic's Flat Potato and Feta Omelet

○ ● ○ ◗ ○ ●

The title says it all: Our indefatigable, ramshackle car broke down as my husband and I drove off the over-night ferry headed for what turned out to be nearly a year on the island of Crete. Our first morning on Crete was spent at a garage in the harbor of Chania, eating breakfast with the mechanic. The car was fixed, and before we headed out for more adventures than we could ever predict, we ate plates of potato and feta cheese omelet, variations of which have stayed with me the rest of my life so far. Add diced salami or sliced sausage—especially if you can find Greek sausages with a whiff of cumin—or, if you like, ditch the feta, add a milder fresh cheese along with a handful of chopped fresh mint, and sprinkle the top with grated *kefalotyri*. As long as you have potatoes and eggs, cooked flat in delicious Greek olive oil, you've got a wonderful dish!

While I call for new small potatoes, such as creamers or Jerseys, any waxy potato works really well in this omelet. If you have only floury potatoes—they brown up nicely, too; omit the parboiling and just slice up thinly, brown in the pan, and add to the eggs.

◇ Serves 2 as a main course for breakfast, lunch, or supper
serves 4 if you'll have other things on the menu

8 to 12 ounces small creamer or new potatoes

Salt and pepper

3 to 5 tablespoons extra-virgin Greek olive oil, or as needed

6 to 8 ounces feta cheese, cut into bite-size chunks

4 large eggs, lightly beaten

2 green onions, cut into thin slices

2 tablespoons coarsely chopped fresh dill, or a large pinch of oregano leaves, crushed between your fingers

1 Parboil the potatoes until they are almost tender; drain, and set aside. When cool enough to handle, slice about 1/4 inch thick, removing as much peel as comes off easily and leaving the rest. Sprinkle with salt and pepper and cool. If you have leftover boiled potatoes, use those and omit this parboiling step.

2 In a heavy nonstick skillet, heat add a tablespoon or two of the olive oil over medium heat, and gently brown the sliced potatoes until they are golden in places. Set aside.

3 Add the feta cheese to the eggs and mix gently; you don't want to break the cheese too much. Then gently add the

continued

continued

browned potatoes to the eggs and cheese. Season to taste with salt and pepper.

4 In a heavy nonstick skillet, heat the remaining olive oil over medium-high heat until it begins to smoke, then gently pour in the egg-potato-feta mixture and smooth out for even distribution.

5 Cook over medium-low heat, every so often pulling up the cooked edges and letting the uncooked egg run down to the bottom of the pan.

6 When the bottom of the omelet is browned golden—take care that you don't burn it—cook the top, which should be slightly soft and runny but not terribly liquidy. You can cook the top by either placing it under the broiler until it puffs lightly and acquires golden flecks here and there, for about 6 minutes, or you can flip it by first loosening all the edges and the bottom with a spatula, then placing an upside-down plate on top, pressing it down gently on the egg mixture, then inverting the whole thing. As long as the eggs are not too liquidy, and the mixture hasn't stuck in the pan, the operation should proceed smoothly. Slide the omelet back into the pan so that the bottom can now brown in the pan; if there is any liquidy melted cheese and egg left on the plate, just push it back into the pan with the rest of the omelet.

7 Cook for about 3 minutes on medium heat, long enough to gild the now bottom of the omelet, and slide onto a plate.

8 Serve cut into wedges, sprinkled with the green onions and dill.

Leah's Potato
and Cheese Scramble

○ ● ○ ● ○ ●

When there is almost nothing in the house to eat, this makes a soothing supper, a cozy brunch, and an almost anytime dish of delicious desperation: Thinly slice potatoes and cook until lightly browned and tender, then pour in beaten eggs and chunks of cheese. Scramble. Mmmmm. The cheese can be any sort of leftover cheese from a cheeseboard selection, tiny bits of this and that, or a delicious cave-aged Gruyère, or a Jack, and one almost always has eggs and some sort of potatoes in the kitchen.

◇ Serves 4

3 large baking or all-purpose white, thin-skinned potatoes (about 12 ounces), peeled or not, as desired

2 to 3 tablespoons extra-virgin olive oil

3 garlic cloves, chopped, or 3 green onions, thinly sliced

6 eggs, lightly beaten together with a tablespoon of water

4 to 6 ounces Gruyère, Monterey, Sonoma Jack, Gouda, *kefalotyri*, Emmentaler, or white Cheddar, diced

Sea salt and freshly ground black pepper

1 Cut the potatoes into very thin slices, as thin as you are able; I prefer a variation of thicknesses and thinnesses, ranging from nearly paper-thin to nearly 1/8 inch thick.

2 Heat the olive oil in a heavy nonstick or cast-iron skillet over medium-high heat until it begins to smoke; make a single layer of potatoes, let them brown slightly, then turn them over and push them to the side into a little pile and make another single layer in the skillet where it is now empty. Repeat, adding a new layer of potatoes each time, so that you end up with all the potatoes browning lightly and evenly. This should take 5 to 10 minutes.

3 Meanwhile, if using garlic, sprinkle it on the potatoes frying in the pan. If using green onions, add them to the beaten eggs.

4 Add the cheese to the eggs. When the potatoes are just tender, pour the egg mixture over the potatoes so that the eggs swoosh around the potatoes and the cheese is evenly distributed. Using a spatula, turn over the edges where the egg has cooked, so that you are scrambling the eggs together with the potatoes and the cheese. The cheese will melt and in some spots sizzle and crisp.

5 When the cheese has melted and the egg has set, remove from the pan, season to taste with salt and pepper, and serve.

Corned Beef Hash
à la James Beard

○ ● ○ ◕ ○ ●

Corned beef hash has long been one of my favorite comfort foods—a good one is sublime (even a bad one is pretty enjoyable). I am, however, picky about my hash: I like it with abundant potatoes and am not fond of other additions besides the basics of corned beef and onions. For instance, I get irrationally aggravated if I'm in a restaurant and I find green bell pepper in my hash, or worst of all, no potatoes!

Here's how this hash became part of my repertoire. When I was first starting to write about food and catering, I took a cooking class with the legendary James Beard. His huge presence sat on a big stool, directing his assistant, the ever-so-sweet Marion Cunningham, who did all the chopping, cutting, frying, and so on, narrating per the Big Man's instructions and comments from the side. I anticipated a lavish feast—he was the leading culinary star of the day, next to Julia Child, and had tasted so many exotic and luxurious foods. Perhaps he'd make something exotic he picked up from Europe, or something sophisticated from New York?

What I got was corned beef hash. And, oh, it was great corned beef hash, accompanied by a pretty nifty coffee cake and citrus compote, too—the menu was brunch—which has traveled with me throughout my corned-beef-and-potato-eating days. The hash that James Beard taught me to make has evolved into "Hash of Whatever Delicious Thing Plus Potatoes" as I've journeyed through life discovering delicious savory meats, sausages, even fish, and finding that most lend themselves deliciously to being turned into hash.

Though the Great One added nutmeg, I prefer a sprinkling of cracked coriander and a scattering of mustard seeds. And he was also a bit more lavish with the cream than I.

By the way, though I call for vegetable oil, and it's fine, if you have any chicken fat (*schmaltz*), or duck or goose fat, lying around your kitchen, toss a little in. You deserve it—I know that I do!

◇ Serves 4

6 large waxy potatoes (about 1½ pounds)

1 medium-large onion, chopped

10 to 12 ounces corned beef, diced (about 2 cups)

1 teaspoon whole coriander seeds, lightly cracked and crushed with a mortar and pestle

Coarse salt and freshly ground black pepper

½ teaspoon mustard seeds

2 to 3 tablespoons vegetable oil, or a mixture of vegetable oil and butter, for browning the hash

2 tablespoons sour cream or heavy (whipping) cream

1 or 2 eggs per person, poached or pan-fried, sunny-side up or over easy

1 Boil the potatoes whole and unpeeled until they are just tender; remove from the heat and let cool. If you have leftover boiled potatoes, this is a good dish to use them in.

2 Cut the potatoes into ¾-inch dice, peeling off as much skin as is easily removed or as much as you want removed. Place the diced potatoes in a large bowl and mix with the onion, corned beef, coriander seeds, salt and pepper to taste, and mustard seeds. Mix together well so that it forms a chunky mass.

3 In a large, nonstick heavy skillet, heat the oil over medium-high heat until it begins to smoke. Spoon the mixture into it, smoothing it down to form a large pancake. Press down, letting it cook undisturbed, until the bottom browns, over medium heat.

4 When the bottom is browned in places, turn using a spatula, and once again let the bottom brown. Spoon on the sour cream evenly, and repeat the browning again once or twice, browning and turning, letting the mixture break up a bit, until you have a mass of browned crusty potatoes and corned beef, along with tender, soft potato-meat mixture. Turn out of the pan and serve right away, along with one or two eggs per person and a pile of toast—rye, sourdough, or whole wheat.

Variations:

Pastrami Hash

Instead of corned beef, use pastrami. Its smoky, peppery taste lends itself to a very savory hash.

Zesty Sausage Hash

Use any of the many delectable sausages available these days, instead of corned beef. Cut the sausages into bite-size morsels and brown before adding to the potato and onion mixture. Try Thai chicken sausage, spicy chipotle or Yucatecan sausage, or merguez, with a large pinch of cumin seeds added to the potato and onion mixture. Sprinkle with chopped cilantro. For Italian sausages, substitute fennel seed and a pinch of oregano for the coriander and mustard seeds and sprinkle with chopped fresh parsley or marjoram. Apple-chicken sausages would be nice, either fresh or smoked; keep the mustard seeds but omit the coriander seeds.

Stovies

A favorite supper of the potato-loving Scots. Substitute an equal amount of sausage, ham, bacon, or a combination of these for the corned beef. Brown them in the pan first and then add the potatoes and onions to the pan, rather than mixing them all together first. Omit the coriander and mustard seeds and the sour cream, but use enough oil to keep the potatoes and meat browning. Cover and cook for about 10 minutes, then turn once or twice and cook uncovered for a further 5 to 10 minutes, or until the meat, onions, and potatoes are browned and crusty in some places, tender and soft in others. Sometimes chicken is included in stovies, or a combination of chicken and bacon or sausage.

Bacon

If you just happen to have bacon fat lurking in your kitchen, use a few judicious spoonfuls to cook these potatoes in.

2

chapter

Tapas, meze, and antipasti are a wonderful way to enjoy afternoon segueing into evening, or to turn a get-together with friends into the evening's entertainment: little plates of savory dishes, in small chunks or pieces; little bites to stab with a fork, or dab at with a piece of bread or vegetable, or pick up with your fingers and pop into your mouth, interspersed with sips of cooling afternoon drinks, or warming wine to start the evening.

Potatoes are fabulous as one of these nibbles, awash in spicy paprika sauce, simmered with olive oil and baked into a tortilla, or fried into a crisp Indian-spiced fritter. These morsels make a fabulous array of textures and tastes. Little nuggets of flavor to jump-start a meal with delight, wake up the palate, and get you purring from pleasure. In addition to the dishes here, many in other chapters make good dishes to serve this way; Salade Russe (page 77) and Kartoffel mit Frankfurter Gruen Sosse (page 84) are both classics, and Latkes (page 144) can always be made in tiny versions. One of my favorite tiny potato morsel dishes was one made by Roland Passot at his wonderfully Gallic San Francisco restaurant, La Folie. Egg cups were filled with a few spoonfuls of teeny tiny diced fingerlings that had been sautéed in butter, then topped with ripe Epoisses cheese and warmed through, the cheese gently melting into a gooshy, unctuous mixture. He topped it with a bit of vinaigrette-dressed frisée—bite into it and get nubbins of potato, a mouthful of melted cheese, and a crisp tangle of frisée, a super-elegant version of the classic French *tartiflette*. He also served an appetizer of a paper-thin piece of carpaccio dressed in truffle oil alongside a tablespoon of potato salad—again, the uber-elegant tiny dice of fingerlings, this time dressed in homemade mayonnaise with shallots. And I love Julia Moskin's bite-size roast potato cylinders, each topped with a dollop of crème fraîche and a spoonful of caviar.

Tapas, meze, and antipasti not only start a meal with zest; they also make great snacks or light meals, and super starters. And like all good tapas, a larger portion can become a main or side dish.

Tapas, Meze & Antipasti

The Olive Presser's Tortilla

○ ● ○ ◖ ○ ●

I was in Andaluciá, the sun-baked southern region of Spain that is home to amazing olive oil
(as well as flamenco), for the local olive harvest. It was also the ninety-first birthday of my host,
the olive grower, who was celebrating by making a massive potato and egg tortilla—the culinary icon
of Spain. Other tortillas are good, but often simply a mixture of potatoes cooked in olive oil
bound with egg; this tortilla—this exaltedly delicious tortilla—is gilded with a layer of peppers and tomatoes,
a tangy contrast to the earthy potatoes and egg. Eat cold, in wedges or squares. The classic tapa of
Spain, tortillas can be prepared in myriad ways— though potato is a great favorite and I always come back
to this tortilla with its flamenco-like topping. (For those with a soft spot in their hearts for
occasional slightly junky/trashy deliciousness, I have heard about a tapas bar that serves tortillas
made from potato chips!) Unlike eggs in the United States, tortillas are not usually served as breakfast
and are seldom eaten hot; rather, they are eaten cool at room temperature,
as a tapa, a snack with a glass of wine, or tucked into a crusty roll as a hearty sandwich.

◇ Serves 6 to 8 as a tapa

5 tablespoons extra-virgin olive oil, or more if needed

4 medium-large baking potatoes, peeled and cut into ½-inch dice

2 medium onions, cut into ½-inch dice

8 garlic cloves, coarsely chopped

Salt and pepper

Large pinch or two of dried thyme, or 1 to 2 tablespoons chopped fresh rosemary

1 red bell pepper, cut into ½-inch dice

1 green bell pepper, cut into ½-inch dice

4 ripe tomatoes, diced (canned is fine)

Tiny pinch of sugar, if needed

About 10 leaves of sweet basil, cut into strips or torn

6 large eggs, lightly beaten

1 In a large nonstick skillet, heat 2 tablespoons of the olive oil over medium heat, and sweat the potatoes and half the onions and garlic. Cook slowly, sprinkling with salt and pepper, covered, until the potatoes and onions are tender and golden-browned here and there, for 10 to 15 minutes. Transfer from the pan to a bowl, season with thyme, and set aside.

2 Add another tablespoon of olive oil to the skillet, and heat over medium-high heat. Lightly sauté the remaining onions and garlic until lightly softened, then add the red and green bell peppers and the tomatoes. Cook down over medium heat until thick and saucy, for 5 to 10 minutes, then season to taste with salt and pepper, and if needed, a tiny pinch of sugar. Transfer from the pan to another bowl and add the basil. Set aside.

3 Combine the potatoes with about three-fourths of the beaten eggs. If you want to bake the tortilla, preheat the oven to 350°F.

4 Heat two more tablespoons of olive oil in the skillet. When the pan is hot, add the potato mixture. If you are cooking on top of the stove, cook over medium-low heat, picking up the edges of the omelet, and letting the liquid flow underneath. If baking, place in the oven for about 20 minutes or long enough to firm it up.

5 When the egg is cooked almost through, place under the broiler to firm up the top; broil for a minute or so, or until the omelet is cooked through but still tender.

6 Meanwhile, mix the pepper-tomato mixture with the remaining egg. When the potato layer is cooked through, pour the mixture over the top and spread it out. Place under the broiler to finish cooking this layer; if baking, return to the oven and bake for a further 10 minutes or until the pepper-tomato layer is cooked through. It may puff up but will flatten again as it cools.

7 Serve at room temperature in little squares or wedges.

Variation:

Saffron-Pea Tortilla with a Blanket of Melted Cheese

Omit the layer with the peppers, tomatoes, and basil, and decrease the eggs to 4.

Prepare the potato-onion-garlic mixture as directed in step 1, cooking until just tender, then combine with the eggs, 25 threads of saffron mixed with a tablespoon of hot water, and 1/2 cup frozen or fresh young, blanched peas. Heat the skillet, wiped clean, with about 2 tablespoons olive oil in it, then pour in the potato-egg-pea mixture and cook over medium-low heat until the bottom is golden and it's firmish all the way up to the top, with just a thin liquidish topping. Place under the broiler, lightly gild, and finish cooking the top, then make a layer of about 6 ounces shredded Jack or Manchego cheese on top. Return to the broiler until melted. Serve hot.

Cazilli

○ ● ○ ● ○ ●

Such a naughty name—oh, yes, it is named after its shape—and such a delicious fritter it is!
Crisp crumbs on the outside, and inside you have mooshy, shmooshy potato studded with bits of ham,
salami, and cheese. Eat cazilli *with glasses of wine as an antipasto or party nibble.*

◇ Serves 4 to 6

1½ pounds large potatoes, either all-purpose, waxy, or floury, unpeeled

3 tablespoons unsalted butter, melted

3 eggs, separated, whites beaten to soft peaks

1½ to 2 ounces diced ham, or lean unsmoked bacon

2 to 3 ounces Italian or French salami, finely diced

2 to 3 tablespoons chopped fresh parsley, preferably flat leaf

6 ounces fontina, or other mild Italian cheese, such as provolone, *caciocavallo*, or mozzarella, diced

½ cup freshly grated Parmesan, Grana Padano, pecorino, Dry Jack, Asiago, or similar cheese

Salt

¼ cup flour, or more as needed

About 2 cups fine bread crumbs, preferably homemade, unseasoned

Oil for pan frying, about ½ inch deep

1 Cook the potatoes in gently boiling salted water until tender. Drain and leave to cool until you can handle them. Holding each potato with a clean dish towel, peel and discard the skin. Mash the potatoes or put through a potato ricer. (I often make this using potatoes that I've boiled a day or two ahead of time, and instead of mashing, I grate them on the large holes of a grater; after you've grated all the flesh, you are left holding most of the skin. You can look at the mixture and pick out any other pieces of errant potato skin lying around.)

2 In a bowl mix the melted butter into the potatoes, then mix in the egg yolks, ham, salami, parsley, fontina, and Parmesan. Season to taste with salt.

3 Shape mixture into 12 cylinders, then dredge each in the flour.

4 Dip each floured cylinder first into the egg white, then into the bread crumbs. Repeat until all the fritters are crumb-coated.

5 Heat the oil in a nonstick heavy skillet over medium-high heat until it just smokes. Carefully add the fritters to the pan, a few at a time, taking care not to crowd the pan (which will lower the temperature of the oil and cause the fritters to turn oily and sodden, or fall apart). The fritters will turn golden brown on one side and should then be turned, and rolled, so that they brown evenly all the way around. You could also deep-fry the fritters, which would eliminate turning them several times.

6 When the fritters are golden brown and crunchy on the outside, use a slotted spoon and remove from the pan; place on absorbent paper and keep hot.

7 Eat right away!

Patatas a la Riojana

○ ● ○ ● ○ ●

Delicious as a tapa, this stew originated in the vineyards of Rioja and was traditionally prepared in the fields during the grape harvest. Either type of chorizo—the salami type for eating or the raw type for cooking—may be used in this recipe.
But there is one more trick, beloved by locals to get just the right consistency of potato and sauce: broken potatoes. Pierce the raw potato with a fork, then pull apart with the fork, letting the potatoes crack and break away. The uneven edges you get from this technique give the sauce a rich thickness and make the consistency of both sauce and potato delightful.

◇ Serves 2 as a modest starter, 6 as a tapa, or 2 as a main course

12 ounces medium-size all-purpose white or floury Russet potatoes, peeled

3 tablespoons extra-virgin olive oil

1 medium-large onion, chopped or cut lengthwise into thin slices

5 garlic cloves, half chopped and half thinly sliced

2 to 3 ounces salami-type chorizo, or 7 ounces sausage chorizo, cut into bite-size pieces

1 to 2 heaping teaspoons Spanish sweet paprika (*pimentón*) (use the larger measurement if using salami-type chorizo, the smaller amount for cooking chorizo)

1 teaspoon white wine vinegar or sherry vinegar

1/2 chicken- or vegetable-flavored bouillon cube, or 1 teaspoon powder

1/4 teaspoon salt

1 Instead of cutting, you are going to be "breaking" the potatoes by piercing them, then breaking them with a fork. Stick the fork in, push it all the way down, then pull the fork sideways and let a chunk of potato break away with it. Repeat. You want the chunks of potato to be in the neighborhood of 1/2 to 2 inches.

2 Heat the olive oil in a heavy several-inches-deep skillet, preferably nonstick, over low to medium-low heat, and cook the onion and the chopped garlic. Cook for about 10 minutes, or until the onion is softened and slightly caramelized in places.

3 Add the chorizo and raise the heat to brown the chorizo in spots; it will give lots of red, flavorful oil to the onion. Then cook for about 5 minutes over medium heat. Add the potatoes and cook through with the chorizo for about 10 minutes.

4 Add the paprika, water to cover, vinegar, bouillon cube, and salt. Raise the heat, bring to a boil, then lower heat slightly and cook over medium heat, turning the potatoes and chorizo every so often, taking care not to mush up or mash the potatoes as they cook. When the sauce has reduced to a thick, intensely flavored red liquid, the potatoes should be tender.

5 Eat as a tapa, a side dish, or a main course. Eat as a midnight snack. Eat for breakfast with eggs. Just eat them.

Tikki Aloo
Indian Potato Fritters

○ ● ○ ◕ ○ ●

Crisp, nutty chickpea batter, with its whiff of Indian spices, cloaks morsels of creamy potato.
These potato fritters are easy to make, and amazingly delicious.

◇ Serves 4

1 pound new potatoes, whole in their skins, preferably Jersey Royals, fingerlings, creamers, or any small potatoes

1 cup chickpea flour

1/2 cup cold water

1/4 to 1/2 teaspoon cumin seeds

1/4 teaspoon asafetida, or as desired

Salt

1/8 to 1/4 teaspoon turmeric

1/2 mild onion, chopped

5 garlic cloves, coarsely chopped or thinly sliced

1/2 teaspoon cumin powder

Pinch of red pepper flakes, or 1/2 to 1 fresh green chile, such as jalapeño or poblano, chopped

Several pinches masala spice mix for onion *bhaji,* or good flavorful curry powder

Olive oil for frying, about 1/2 inch deep

Wedges of lime and coarse salt, or chutney, or yogurt *raita* (dipping sauce), for garnishing

1 In a saucepan large enough to fit them, place the potatoes with salted water to cover. Bring to a boil, then reduce the heat to a gentle simmer. Cook until they are just tender, for about 10 to 15 minutes. Remove from the heat and drain.

2 Meanwhile, place the chickpea flour in a bowl and slowly add the cold water, whisking with a wire whisk as you do. Continue to whisk until the mixture is a smooth, thickish cream. Add cumin seeds and asafetida, and season to taste with salt. Set aside.

3 When the potatoes are cool enough to handle, coarsely break apart using a fork. Mix them with turmeric, onion, garlic, cumin, red pepper flakes, and masala. Toss together. Stir the chickpea flour mixture; it may have thickened while it was sitting. If it seems thicker than a thick paste or cream, add a tablespoon or two of water, then stir until smooth. Stir the chickpea mixture into the potato mixture.

4 Heat the olive oil in a heavy skillet, preferably nonstick, over medium-high heat. When the oil is hot and ready for frying, make pancakes with about 2 tablespoons of the chickpea-potato batter. Fry until the bottom is golden and the mixture is cooked through. Turn and cook until golden brown and crisp on the second side.

5 Transfer the pancake-fritters with a slotted spoon to a platter lined with absorbent paper.

6 Serve with wedges of lime and a pile of coarse salt, or with either a chutney or a yogurt *raita.*

Rosemary Roast Potatoes
with Black Olive-Rosemary Aioli

○ ● ○ ◗ ○ ●

Salty-crispy-herby on the outside, they are creamy within. If you find teeny tiny baby potatoes—
often called marbles—at the farmers' market, use these and omit the step of boiling; simply roast.
The dipping sauce is deliciously spunky and, at the risk of sounding trite, they are, if not addictive, then
just plain hard to stop eating. In addition to the Black Olive–Rosemary Aioli, you might also consider
Romescu Sauce (page 50) or Saffron Aioli (page 142). If you can't be bothered making a sauce
at all, a bowl of Greek yogurt sprinkled with sliced green onions is delish, too.

◇ Serves 4 to 6 as a tapa

1½ pounds small waxy potatoes, unpeeled

1 or 2 tablespoons extra-virgin olive oil

Coarse sea salt for sprinkling

2 to 3 tablespoons chopped fresh rosemary leaves, plus a few sprigs for garnish

Black Olive–Rosemary Aioli (recipe follows)

1 Preheat the oven to 375°F to 400°F. Meanwhile, place the potatoes in a saucepan with salted water to cover. Bring to a boil, then cook over medium-high heat until they are about half-way tender. This will depend on the size of the potatoes, but will be generally between 6 and 10 minutes. Drain, then toss with the olive oil, sea salt, and half the rosemary.

2 Arrange the potatoes in a baking dish in a single layer and roast in the oven for about 30 minutes or until the potatoes are golden and crispy. Turn with a spatula once or twice as needed.

3 Toss with the reserved rosemary and enjoy either hot or at room temperature with Black Olive–Rosemary Aioli for dipping, if you like.

Black Olive–Rosemary Aioli

A creative adaptation of both the French aioli and the Greek *skorthalia*, the addition of olives and rosemary lends a fragrant presence. Using store-bought mayonnaise as a base makes it so easy that it's silly.

◇ Makes about 1 1/2 cups

2 to 3 garlic cloves, chopped

3 to 4 tablespoons black olive paste, or more as needed

1 tablespoon chopped fresh rosemary leaves

4 tablespoons mayonnaise, or more as desired or needed

4 to 6 tablespoons extra-virgin olive oil

Juice of 1/4 lemon

1 In a bowl, stir together the garlic, olive paste, and rosemary. Then beat in the mayonnaise.

2 When it's smooth and thick, add the olive oil a little bit at a time, letting the mixture thicken and the oil to absorb, then adding a little more. You may do this with a whisk, a spoon, or in a food processor. Add more olive paste if it needs a stronger olive flavor.

3 Add lemon juice to taste, and chill until ready to serve. May be kept in the refrigerator for up to 3 days.

Bibeleskaes

○ ● ○ ◕ ○ ●

From Alsace, France's region that borders Germany, and sometimes served as a starter or nibble, sometimes as the meal itself, this potato feast consists of a bowl of hot boiled small potatoes, such as creamers, new potatoes, or fingerlings, accompanied by a bowl of *fromage blanc* with chopped onions or shallots, chives, parsley, garlic, tarragon, and chervil, and sometimes a plate of prosciutto or other dry, air-cured ham.

I like to serve the cheese ready-mixed with aromatics, so that the ingredients all have time to meld together. This dish is about the lovely cheese spread, yes, but it's all about the potatoes; so only make it when your potatoes are terrific—small, earthy, and fragrant.

◇ Serves 6 as a tapa, 4 as a starter

12 ounces *fromage blanc* or *fromage frais*, or 8 ounces cottage cheese puréed and mixed with 4 ounces crème fraîche or sour cream

3 ounces unsalted butter at room temperature

1/4 medium white onion, chopped, 1 to 2 shallots, or 3 to 4 green onions, thinly sliced

1 to 2 garlic cloves, chopped

1 to 2 tablespoons dry white wine

1 tablespoon chopped fresh parsley

1 tablespoon chopped fresh tarragon

1 to 2 teaspoons chopped fresh dill or chervil

1 tablespoon chopped chives or green onion tops

Salt and pepper

1 1/2 pounds small heirloom-variety new potatoes, such as Jersey Royals, small fingerlings, or La Ratte

1 Whisk or beat the *fromage blanc* with the butter, then mix in the onion, garlic, wine, parsley, tarragon, dill, and chives. Season to taste with salt and pepper. Place in a bowl or in a jar that has been lined with cheesecloth. After the cheesecloth has been filled, pull up the ball of cheese somewhat and hang it in the bowl from a lid, or tie it around a big spoon. You want the liquid to drain into the bowl. Cover and chill for about 12 hours.

2 Cook the potatoes whole, unpeeled, in salted gently boiling water. When they are just tender, after about 10 minutes, remove from the heat and drain. Sprinkle them lightly with salt and return the pan to the heat, shaking to flip the potatoes over, while you dry them over low to medium heat. When the water has disappeared and the potatoes are not yet scorched, remove them from the pan. They will have evaporated their excess water and taken on an almost sealike briny flavor from the sprinkled salt.

3 Remove the cheese from the refrigerator. Pull the cheese mixture in its little cloth bag out of the bowl, and discard the liquid left behind. Serve the cheese in a ceramic bowl, and the hot potatoes alongside. To eat, take a hot potato and a dab of the cheese mixture, and eat together as you desire.

Patatas a la Importancia

This is a traditional Sevillana tapa: Large slices of potatoes sandwich a layer of cheese; the parcels are then dipped in egg and flour, and fried. Serve drenched in a tangy sauce of garlic, parsley, and white wine.

◇ Serves 4 as a hearty tapa

Potato Sandwiches

2 large floury baking-type potatoes such as russet (6 to 8 ounces each), peeled

8 ounces Emmentaler or Appenzeller cheese, cut into thin slices

Salt

4 tablespoons olive oil, for frying, adding more as needed

2 eggs, beaten, for coating

4 tablespoons flour, for coating, adding more as needed

Sauce

2 tablespoons extra-virgin olive oil

10 garlic cloves, thinly sliced

1 bunch parsley (flat leaf or curly leaf), chopped

2 tablespoons flour

1½ cups dry, nicely acidic white wine

Salt

1 To make the potato sandwiches: Thinly slice, lengthwise, the potatoes, about ¼ to ½ inch thick.

2 Pairing the potato slices by their size, make sandwiches, filling the inside with the sliced cheese. Sprinkle with salt to taste.

3 Preheat the oven to 375°F.

4 Heat the olive oil in a heavy nonstick skillet over medium-highish heat. Dip each sandwich first into the beaten egg, then into the flour, then into the hot oil. Repeat until the pan is filled, cooking the potato sandwiches in batches. Cook until the bottom of the potato sandwiches are golden and flecked with brown. Turn, keeping the sandwiches together. If a sandwich falls apart, reform it after you turn it.

5 As each sandwich is cooked through, transfer to a baking pan, in a single layer, and add more potato sandwiches to the skillet. When all the potatoes are cooked through, place the baking pan in the oven and bake for the 5 to 8 minutes it will take to make the sauce.

6 To make the sauce: Rinse the skillet of the browned and by now slightly burned flour bits; return the pan to the stove and heat over medium-high heat.

7 Add the olive oil and garlic and warm through; when it turns slightly golden, add the parsley and stir together with the garlic until the parsley is slightly wilted and green with the oil. Sprinkle with the flour, and cook, stirring, for several minutes, to cook out the rawness of the flour.

8 Add about half the wine, and stir over the heat, letting the sauce thicken, then keep adding the wine until you have a smooth sauce and some of the harsh alcoholic flavor is burned away. Season to taste with salt.

9 Remove the potato sandwiches from the oven, arrange on a platter, and pour the sauce over them. Serve right away.

Grilled Marinated Potato Slices
with Whole Green Onions
and Romesco Sauce

○ ● ○ ◗ ○ ◗

Slices of meaty, earthy potatoes, preboiled for inner fluffiness, brushed with an extra-virgin olive oil marinade, and grilled to utter crispness. Barbecuing slabs—steaks, really— of lightly boiled, marinated floury potatoes gives a delicious result, like no other.

Serve with whole green onions if you like, and Romesco Sauce, the traditional Catalan accompaniment to the onions. But truthfully, you could also serve these delicious potatoes with Saffron Aioli (with or without the saffron) to go with the thin wafers of potatoes (page 140), garlicky enough to rock your socks off!

◇ Serves 4 to 6

1½ pounds large baking potatoes, such as russet, peeled
Salt and pepper
1 to 2 tablespoons fresh thyme leaves
Juice of ½ lemon
½ cup extra-virgin olive oil, as needed
1 bunch green onions, trimmed to tidy up the rough ends
Romesco Sauce (following page)

1 Parboil the potatoes in salted water to cover at a gently simmering boil, until they are half cooked: tender on the outside but a bit crunchy when you reach the center. Drain and set aside.

2 When cool enough to handle, slice the potatoes lengthwise into steaks about ½- to ¾-inch thick, taking care to keep the potatoes in big thick slices; do not let them fall apart unnecessarily or they will fall through the spaces on the grill of the barbecue. Sprinkle with salt, pepper, thyme, and lemon juice, and then drizzle lightly with olive oil as needed. Set aside.

3 Heat the barbecue or stovetop grill; when hot, barbecue the potato slices and whole green onions, until they are charred here and there, and tender but not overcooked.

4 Serve the hot grilled potatoes and green onions with the Romesco Sauce.

Romesco Sauce

I do sometimes include the skins of the garlic cloves in a very rustic sauce. It's easier and the food processor relegates them to mush; any pieces of skin can just be lifted out. I've heard that countryside cooks in the Mediterranean say you can taste the difference when the skins are pounded along with the flesh.

½ cup extra-virgin olive oil, as needed

3 to 4 tablespoons fresh bread crumbs

3 to 4 garlic cloves, unpeeled

¼ cup dry-roasted almonds

3 tomatoes, fire-roasted (from a can is fine, otherwise roast over a barbecue or under a broiler until the skin is charred and the tomatoes collapse)

½ to 1 red bell pepper, fire-roasted

¼ to ½ teaspoon chile powder, such as ancho or New Mexican

½ teaspoon Spanish sweet paprika (*pimentón*)

About ¼ cup tomato juice (from the tomatoes you have used, or bottled)

1 to 2 teaspoons sherry vinegar

Salt

1 In a heavy skillet, heat a tablespoon or two of the olive oil and toast the bread crumbs until they are lightly golden and crisp. Remove from the heat and leave to cool.

2 In a food processor, purée the garlic, then add the almonds and purée them into a fine-ish mix. Add the bread crumbs and whirl again; it will be a gritty mixture. Add the tomatoes, red bell pepper, chile powder, and paprika, and whirl together until it thickens; add enough of the tomato juice to give it a juicy, creamy consistency, then gradually add a few tablespoons of the olive oil, as desired. It should be a thick, emulsified sauce.

3 Add the vinegar and salt to taste, and whirl again. Add a few tablespoons of cold water if the mixture needs smoothing out, or another slosh of vinegar or tomato juice if the mixture needs either a tart edge or a tomato sweetness. Chill until ready to use.

Chermoula Potatoes

○ ● ○ ◉ ○ ●

Mmmmmm, chunks or slices of creamy new potatoes or fingerlings, tossed with a green purée of garlicky cilantro, chiles, and preserved lemon, a dressing known in Morocco as *chermoula*. This is spunky and tangy, perfect to stimulate you when you're feeling jaded from the heat and a little blasé about life.

Charming Moroccan food writer Chimicha Achanki and her equally charming husband, Karim, inspired this dish by sharing with me fragrant spices and homemade preserved lemon, as well as lots of tasty ideas!

Serve with toothpicks to pick out chunks of the potatoes, or on a little plate as part of a selection of tapas.

◇ Serves 4

1½ pounds small white-skinned new potatoes, such as fingerlings or kidney-shaped new potatoes

Salt

Chermoula (recipe follows)

1 Cook the potatoes by placing them in a heavy saucepan with salted water to cover. Bring to a boil, then reduce the heat, cover, and simmer for about 10 minutes or until the potatoes are just tender. Pour off the water, cover, and set aside while you make the *chermoula*.

2 Slice the cooked potatoes thickly, or cut into large bite-size pieces. Peel if you like, or just peel partially—I find this the easiest way—you get the taste benefits of peeling, without the fiddly nature of pulling all the skin away.

3 Toss the potatoes gently with the green *chermoula*, taking care not to mash or break up the potatoes.

4 Enjoy at room temperature.

Chermoula

5 garlic cloves, coarsely chopped

1 to 1½ small or medium fresh medium-hot chile, red or green, cut up

½ to ¾ cup loosely packed cilantro leaves

½ to 1 teaspoon ground cumin

3 tablespoons extra-virgin olive oil

½ to 1 teaspoon capers, preferably salt-cured and unrinsed, or brine-packed and unrinsed

¼ teaspoon curry powder, or *raz al hanout* powder

¼ teaspoon ground ginger

½ to 1 preserved lemon

Juice of 1 medium to large lemon or lime

Salt, if needed

1 In a food processor, whirl the garlic with the chile, cilantro, cumin, and olive oil, then whirl in the capers, curry powder, and ginger.

2 Cut the preserved lemon into halves and remove the flesh. Rinse the peel under cold running water, then add it to the green purée; stir in the lemon or lime juice. Be sure to taste before seasoning with more salt—capers and preserved lemons are both salty.

3

Potato

Basically, if you cook potatoes in lots of water or broth, you have soup. My grandmother would cook waxy potatoes together with scraps of smoked salmon and serve it in soup bowls with a dollop of sour cream, and a sprinkling of green onions. Delish. My husband's mother simmered potatoes in a pot of consommé with chunks of tender beef, until the potatoes fell into tender pieces. In Germany I recently spooned up a soup of potato chunks simmered in a rich onion and marjoram broth, splashed with a bit of cream.

Once you've cooked potatoes with the basics, gild with cream and butter, add handfuls of herbs, or enrich them with a handful of vegetables, little meatballs, tangy yogurt, leafy greens, sunny tomatoes; potato soup varies endlessly, but at its heart it is simply cooked potatoes and their liquid. And it's delicious.

You can purée potato soup into a luxurious bowlful and float a pat of herbed or porcini-flavored butter on top; you can add a couple of cold boiled potatoes to hot borscht, or some hot potatoes to cold borscht (either way, the soup flavor is absorbed into the delicious bland potato). You can make a small piece of meat and a few spoonfuls of paprika, along with a bag of potatoes, into a hearty goulash. In other words, you could eat potato soup every day, every evening, and probably by the end of the year you would still be making new soups.

For a soup lover, all soups are good. But potato soup—mmmmm, that's bliss.

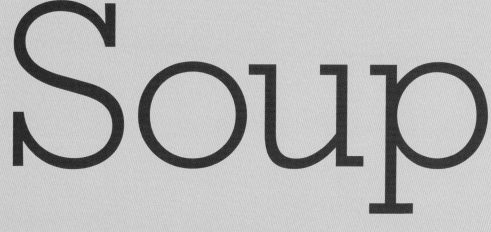

Soup

Potato Soup Inspirations

French Family Supper Soup: Add a big floury potato, peeled and diced, to any vegetable soup meant to be puréed; potatoes add a creamy richness to the pot. Thick carrot, earthy artichoke, or spinach and potato soup—yum!

Broth of Spicy Clarity, with Potato: To a clear broth, such as Mexican seafood, clear borscht, or Mediterranean fish soup, add sliced or whole boiled potatoes and warm through. They won't thicken the broth; rather, the lovely potato morsels will add body to an otherwise light, liquidy soup. I like diced cooked potatoes added to puréed tomato soup, Mexican style, with a hit of chipotle salsa. Ditto for Indian subcontinent spices.

Anywhere on Earth Potato and Lentil Soup: Add peeled, diced floury potatoes to any soup made with legumes, such as lentil soup or split pea soup, to thicken it in a relaxed, uneven way. You'll end up with some thickening, as well as morsels of potatoes, too.

A Bowl of Many Potatoes from the Andes: In Colombia and Peru, both waxy and floury potatoes are simmered together in one soup, the waxy ones to keep their shapes, the floury ones to thicken the sauce. Far away, in potato-loving Ireland, they do this too!

Dumplings, dumplings everywhere!: Either potato dumplings from Eastern Europe or gnocchi from Italy (page 164) are delicious in any soup, not just consommé—onion, goulash, minestrone, tomato, and basil. It's dumplings without borders!

Tranquility with French Fries, Miso Soup: Add a handful of thick french fries (made from floury, not too sweet, potatoes), broken or cut into smaller lengths, along with thinly sliced green onion and a few optional shreds of ham to a bowl of hot, savory miso broth (dissolve a spoonful or two of miso in vegetable, fish, or chicken broth, or use a packet of dried miso soup).

Creamy Potato and Cheese Soup from the Swiss Mountains: So delicious you may wish to yodel. Leftover mashed potatoes make a delicious cheesy soup. Stir a cup or so into hot chicken or vegetable broth and cook, stirring, until the mixture is thickened; add a half cup or so of cream, then ladle it over a handful of grated Gruyère or Emmentaler cheese in your bowl, and sprinkle the top with thinly sliced green onions.

Minestra al Orzo
Italian Alpine Soup of Broccoli, Barley, and Potato

○ ● ○ ◗ ○ ●

You can make this Alpine soup with nettles or any other wild green you find in the farmers' market or foraging on an afternoon's walk.

This is even better prepared a day before it is to be eaten. If you do use nettles instead of broccoli, allow a longer cooking time for the nettles to become soft and tender, and for them to lose their ability to sting (the irritating sting is from tiny hairs, which are rendered harmless through cooking).

◇ Serves 4 to 6

2 tablespoons olive oil, or duck or goose fat

1 onion, chopped

4 garlic cloves, sliced

¼ cup barley

2 to 3 bay leaves

3 cups broth

3 cups water

3 medium-small waxy potatoes (12 ounces), peeled and cut into two-bite-size chunks

Half a head of broccoli, cut into bite-size pieces

Salt and pepper

Grated Parmesan, pecorino, Grana Padano, or other grating cheese

1 In a heavy soup pot, heat the olive oil over medium-high heat and lightly sauté the onion and garlic until softened. Add the barley, bay leaves, broth, and water, and cook over medium heat for about 40 minutes or until the barley is almost tender.

2 Add the potatoes and continue cooking, covered, until the potatoes are tender and falling apart in places.

3 Add the broccoli and cook until tender, for about 5 minutes; season with salt and pepper to taste.

4 Ladle into bowls and eat, sprinkled with grated cheese.

Potato and Leek Soup
from the Highlands of Scotland

○ ● ○ ◐ ○ ●

This is a classic soup of France and also a favorite in the Highlands of Scotland, due no doubt to the Auld Alliance. Its French name, Potage Parmentier, is a tribute to Antoine-Auguste Parmentier, who convinced France that the potato is safe—and delicious—to eat.

Once my Scottish husband took me on a potato pilgrimage to Scotland. His parents had grown potatoes and waxed lyrical about the glories of those from Ayr, so we took a flight, rented a car, and headed into the countryside, hell-bent for taters. The Ayrshire potatoes were fabulous, so earthy and fine; I bought a bag. (Was I the only airplane passenger schlepping a ten-pound bag of potatoes? I was, but I hasten to add that it was well within the weight restrictions of the flight.)

Serve the soup chunky, with a dab of crème fraîche swirled in, or whip it up in the blender with a splash of cream for a smooth, tantalizing green-flecked purée. Chunky or smooth, it's best hot. To eat it cool, though, whirl until smooth and creamy, and you'll have the fancy-schmancy and ever-so-tasty vichyssoise; whirl it with a big handful of fresh watercress and a few leaves of cooked and squeezed-dry spinach and you have a verdant, bright green cream, a peasant soup at its aristocratic best with a dab of crème fraîche and a spoonful of gray-black or glistening gold-red caviar.

◇ Serves 4

3 medium to large leeks, trimmed of their root ends and their rough, scraggly green ends, keeping as much of the tender green leaves as possible

12 ounces flavorful white, preferably baking, potatoes, peeled and diced

6 cups chicken or vegetable broth or stock

Salt and black pepper

1/3 to 1/2 cup crème fraîche

2 tablespoons chopped chives

1 Place the leeks and potatoes in a saucepan with the broth. Bring to a boil, then reduce the heat and simmer, covered, over medium to medium-low heat until the potatoes and leeks are cooked and falling apart, for about 15 minutes, depending on the cooking temperature and how large or small the pieces are cut.

2 Season to taste with salt and pepper, then swirl in the crème fraîche and heat through.

3 For a chunky soup, ladle it into bowls while still hot, and garnish each with a sprinkling of chives. For a smooth soup, whirl
in the food processor until smooth, and pass through a sieve for
extra smoothness. Serve hot or cold, sprinkled with chives.

Variations:

Hot Potato and Leek Soup

Serve the potato and leek soup hot; omit the crème fraîche,
add a few tablespoons cream or whole milk instead, and
into each bowl of hot soup place a few slices of raw
Spanish chorizo, to melt in alluringly.

Watercress and Potato Bisque

Omit leeks and add 2 chopped garlic cloves to the simmering
potatoes and broth, as well as a handful of spinach during the
last few moments. Replace crème fraîche with 1$^{1}/_{2}$ cups heavy
(whipping) cream, and whirl the soup with 1 bunch of coarsely
chopped watercress until it forms a creamy green purée.

Season to taste with salt and pepper, and add a drop or two of
lemon juice to sharpen the flavor. Serve either hot or cold, with
a scattering of chives. For gorgeousness and lavishness, top
each bowl of soup with a dollop of crème fraîche and a spoonful
of sleek black or chunky red salmon caviar.

Parisian Radish-Leaf Potage

Add a handful of radish tops (1 large or 2 medium bunches,
coarsely chopped) to the hot soup just before whirling to a
purée. Don't add the créme fraîche; instead, serve each bowl
with a spoonful on top, and a little bit of grated or thinly sliced
radish, too, for color and texture.

Potato-Cauliflower Soup

○ ● ○ ● ○ ●

Rich and creamy, with the scent of Alba's finest truffle, this soup is a decadent joy to sip on a cold autumn night. If you don't feel like making *croûtes*—large croutons or slices of toasted bread—omit, and simply add a spoonful of the truffle paste to each bowlful. Don't stir; let each person spoon up the soup, adding little bits of the truffle essence with each mouthful of creamy soup. Be careful, though; truffles—especially white ones—are considered an aphrodisiac. (Don't say you weren't warned.)

◇ Serves 4 to 6

Croûtes

4 to 6 thickish slices sourdough country bread, or 8 to 12 slices baguette

Olive oil for drizzling

1 large or 2 small to medium baking potatoes, peeled and cut into large chunks or thick slices

1 small or 1/2 medium cauliflower, cut into florets

4 cups rich chicken, beef, or vegetable broth

1 cup heavy (whipping) cream

1/2 to 1 teaspoon white truffle paste, truffle and porcini paste, truffle and black olive paste, or truffle and asparagus paste

1 To make the *croûtes*: Heat the oven to 350°F. Arrange the sliced bread on a baking sheet and drizzle lightly or brush with olive oil. Bake for about 15 minutes or until light and toasty. Turn over and repeat until the bread is crunchy. Remove from the oven and set aside.

2 In a large saucepan, combine the potatoes, cauliflower, and broth. Bring to a boil, then reduce the heat to medium and cook until the vegetables are tender.

3 Remove from the heat. With a slotted spoon, transfer the vegetables to a food processor or blender, and whirl to make a smooth purée, adding enough of the liquid for smoothness. You could also use a hand-held blender to purée the soup. For a silkier, smoother texture, put the mixture through a tamis or sieve. Return the puréed mixture to the pot along with the remaining broth.

4 Add the cream to the soup and heat together.

5 Serve the hot soup in individual bowls. Spread each *croûte* with the truffle paste and float one on top of each bowl of soup. Serve right away.

Polish Pickle Soup

○ ● ○ ● ○ ●

Potatoes and pickles are a match made in heaven, as generations of my Eastern European ancestors would have known, though I don't remember any grandparents, or aunts and uncles, taking me aside and imparting this important life-enhancing advice: put potatoes and pickles together and you have a heck of a soup! (It's also a pretty wonderful combination for salad, as Salade Russe [page 77] will attest to.)

You can vary this soup hugely: make it with meat broth or vegetable broth—the only ingredients you really need are potatoes and pickles, though fresh dill does oomph up the flavor, and the cream, well, the cream gives it that naughty happy feeling. I generally use a kosher dill that has a whiff of vinegar in it, rather than a more artisanal and traditionally homemade type, the kind based only on salt brine, to start the fermentation. The vinegar is important in this soup for its tanginess; you could also use a Polish dill, or ordinary dill pickle.

◇ Serves 4 to 6

8 medium-size waxy potatoes (about 1½ pounds), cut into 1-inch chunks

1½ to 2 medium carrots, cut into small dice

1 stalk celery, including some of the leaves, chopped

2 cups low-salt broth

1 cup water

2 cups heavy (whipping) cream

2 dill pickles (I prefer kosher dills), shredded or finely chopped, plus about ¼ cup of their own brine

¼ to ½ cup coarsely chopped fresh dill (about half a bunch)

Salt and freshly ground black pepper

1 Combine the potatoes, carrots, and celery in a pot with the broth and water. Cook until the carrots are still bright orange and full of flavor, and the potatoes just tender, for 15 to 25 minutes. Add the cream and warm through for about 5 minutes.

2 Stir in the pickles and pickle brine, then warm through and cook for about 5 minutes.

3 Stir in the chopped dill; season to taste with salt and pepper. In lieu of salt, I often just add a little extra pickle brine.

Variation:

Winter in Poland Soup

If celery root (celeriac) is in season (autumn and winter), I'll add a chunk, peeled and diced, instead of the chopped celery. Add to the pot when you cook the carrot and potatoes, since it takes celeriac as long to cook as it does potatoes, sometimes even longer. Adding celeriac instead of celery makes the soup even more hearty and warming.

South Indian Potato-Coconut Soup

○ ● ○ ● ○ ●

*Pale pink from the tomatoes and thick from simmered potato and coconut, this is a simple
and yet complex soup, fragrant and silky smooth and very rich. You must make it with no further delay!*

◇ Serves 4 as a first course or light lunch,
12 to 16 in tiny demitasse cups for a starter or canapé

1 tablespoon butter

1 teaspoon cumin seeds

Pinch of asafetida

**1 pound potatoes, peeled and diced (any type of potato
is fine)**

2 ripe medium-large tomatoes, diced (including their juices)

Salt and pepper

2 cups vegetable broth

2 cups coconut milk

Ground cumin, for sprinkling, as needed

1 In a heavy-bottomed saucepan, melt the butter and lightly toast the cumin seeds, sprinkling in the asafetida as you do. When the seeds begin to pop, add the potatoes and tomatoes and their juices, and cook together over medium-low heat for several minutes until the tomatoes begin to turn saucy. Sprinkle with salt and pepper as they cook.

2 Add the broth, and bring to a boil over high heat. Reduce the heat to a low simmer, and cook until the potatoes are tender, for about 20 minutes.

3 Purée the potatoes either by mashing with a masher, passing through a sieve, blending with a hand-held blender, or using a food processor. Return to the pot, and stir in the coconut milk over medium-low heat, stirring until blended. Add a little extra water—up to about a cup—if soup is too thick or condensed in flavor; warm through with the rest of the mixture.

4 Taste for seasoning, and add a little sprinkling of ground cumin to boost the cumin seed flavor, if needed. Serve right away.

Aqua Cotta
Garlicky Potato-Tomato Broth with Arugula
from the Maremma in Tuscany

○ ● ○ ◉ ○ ●

Aqua cotta literally means "cooked water." This could be because the soup is old and traditional, of a time when any soup made without meat stock was merely water—hence the name.
Of course, the water (or vegetable or chicken broth) is cooked with lovely rough foods, depending on the garden of the moment; in this version, it's pungent leaves of arugula, sunny tomatoes, and earthy potatoes all awash with fragrant garlic and olive oil.

It is fabulous for lunch, each bite the very essence of Tuscany.

◇ Serves 4 as a light dish for lunch, or starter for a larger meal

2 tablespoons extra-virgin olive oil

6 garlic cloves, thinly sliced, plus 2 extra garlic cloves cut into halves, for rubbing on the stale bread

1 cup diced tomatoes (canned is fine, including the juice)

1 cup dry white wine

2 medium-size potatoes (about 10 ounces), cooked, peeled, and sliced about 3/4 inch thick (if large, first cut lengthwise into halves or quarters)

Small pinch of red pepper flakes

5 cups chicken or vegetable broth

Several big handfuls arugula leaves, preferably the wild spindly type, coarsely chopped

4 thick slices stale or lightly toasted bread, preferably sourdough

1 In a large, heavy nonreactive saucepan, heat the olive oil over medium heat and cook the sliced garlic until lightly golden, then add the tomatoes and their juice and cook for a few minutes more. Pour in the wine, cook over medium-high heat until the liquid has almost completely evaporated, then add the potatoes and red pepper flakes, stir together for a few minutes, then pour in the broth.

2 Cook over medium heat for about 15 minutes.

3 Just before serving, add the arugula and rub the bread with the additional cut cloves of garlic.

4 Into each bowl place a piece of garlic-rubbed bread, ladle over the soup, and serve.

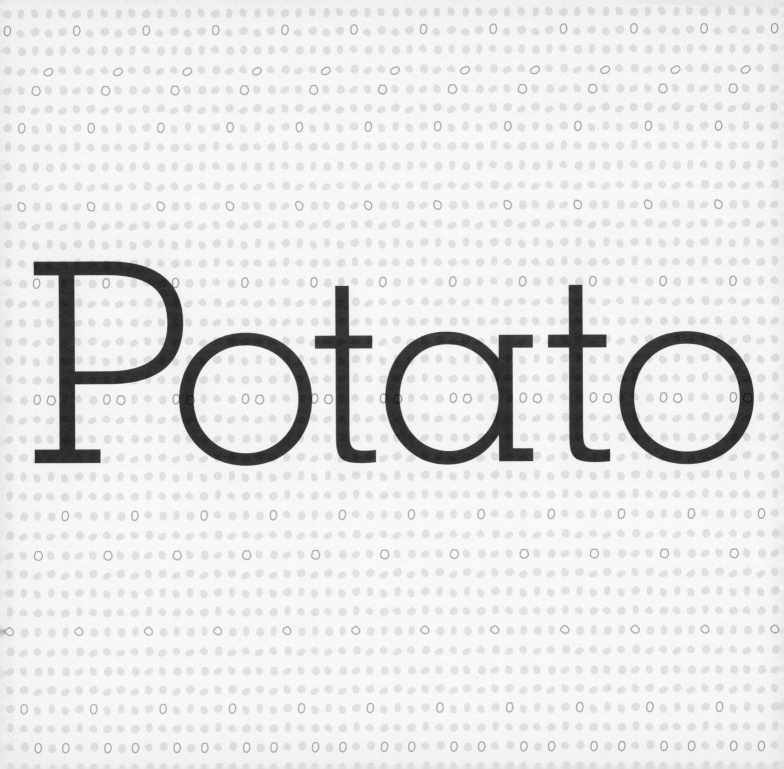

chapter 4

Salad

Marlena's desert-island comfort food: a bowl of potato salad.

My life is full of potato salads, resplendent with potato salads, too many potato salads for one person, for one lifetime, for one neighborhood, one city, one continent. And I love them all!

Soothed with mayonnaise or aioli, finished with a bit of tart sour cream or thick yogurt, or tangy in a dressing based on a mustardy vinaigrette. In fact, simply boil up some waxy potatoes, splash them with a bit of extra-virgin olive oil, and you are well on your way to a salad. I even love many store-bought potato salads—some are fine on their own; others need to be perked up with additions of herbs, spices, or other goodies.

Simple Potato Salads

Slice peeled boiled waxy potatoes. Dress with a drizzle of extra-virgin olive oil and one of the following variations:

Magreb-Flavor Potato Salad: Sprinkle with garlic, cumin, and cilantro and add a big squirt of lemon juice along with a dab of harissa chile paste. A few chunks of salty white cheese is good with this too, or a sprinkling of diced pink pickled turnips *(torshi)*.

Hooray, I'm in Italy Potato Salad: Add several green onions, thinly sliced, and a shake of white wine vinegar, salt, and pepper.

Mittel-Europa Potato Salad: Sprinkle while still warm with dry white wine, then a mustardy vinaigrette. Serve with herring or slabs of cooked spicy sausage (preferably German or Eastern European) on the side, and lots of chopped onion!

Potato Salad from the Cobbled Streets of Vieux Nice: Add green beans, black olives, and a dollop of aioli. Close your eyes; smell the garlic; think of France.

Patata Salata Olivata: Olivey potato salad. Dress with extra-virgin olive oil to which a spoonful of black olive paste or tapenade has been added, giving it salty little olivey flecks.

Potatoes with Moorish Flavors: Like a Matisse palette of color and a flamenco dance of taste. Dress the sliced olive oil–dressed potatoes with a squirt of lime, then dot with tiny cubes of cooked beet, and halves of yellow and red cherry tomatoes. Sprinkle with cumin or hot smoked paprika, then scatter with cilantro, thinly sliced green onions, and fresh dill. Garnish with a handful of oil-cured black olives.

Amalfi Coast Potato and Tomato Salad with Tuna: In late summer when tomatoes are at their ripe, sweet, tangy best, scatter them, sliced or in wedges, around the potatoes, along with shreds of sweet red onion and chunks of tuna packed in olive oil. Dress with white wine vinegar, salt to taste, a sprinkling of capers, and a big pinch of dried oregano or fresh basil leaves. Scatter with arugula leaves, and, if the mood strikes you, a couple of hard-cooked eggs cut into wedges.

Summertime and the Livin' Is Easy Potato Salad: This one is from the Greek island of Corfu. Add thinly sliced, parboiled or roasted green bell peppers, wine vinegar, and chopped parsley.

Winter on the Greek Island of Cephalonia with Potatoes: Dress with a tangy mustard-wine dressing, then garnish with several spoonfuls of just-cooked brown lentils and a little ham, parsley, and onion.

Another Greek Island, Yet Another Potato Salad: Serve the olive oil–lashed potatoes with lots of lemon, green onions, and fresh dill. Catch a fish from the sea and cook it over the grill to eat alongside.

Live the Life of Luxury: Garnish the sliced waxy potatoes with morsels of cooked lobster meat. Dress in olive oil or nut vinaigrette; garnish with chives, chervil, and a handful of baby greens.

Mauricio Asta's Buenos Aires Papa-Tatay Salad to Eat with Barbecued Meat: Cut about 1 pound peeled, boiled, cooled, creamy-fleshed waxy potatoes into bite-size pieces or large dice. Mash 6 to 8 tablespoons cream cheese with an equal amount of mayonnaise and an equal amount—or even more—chopped flat-leaf parsley. I add about 4 thinly sliced green onions, too, and salt and pepper to taste.

Rustic Flavors of Southwest France: Make this and save a little bit to share with your truffle hound. Add a little chopped garlic, a spoonful or two of dry white wine, and a few shakes of truffle oil. Garnish with warm garlicky cooked sausage.

Happiness Is a Warm Potato: Serve the olive oil–dressed potatoes warm, topped with a dollop or two of Greek yogurt or Middle Eastern *laban*, as well as a scattering of thinly sliced preserved lemon. Sprinkle with paprika.

Hakim's Mother's Potato Salad for a Monsoon Day: Bake your potatoes in the ashes of a fire if possible; otherwise bake them slowly until very dry inside. Scoop out the interiors, then discard the skins. Mash the potato lightly, so that some is mashed and some is left in chunks. Toss with thinly sliced shallots and chopped cilantro, and moisten it all with mustard oil; season with sea salt and dried red pepper flakes. Eat and enjoy even though it's raining buckets outside.

Herta Peju's Ausician Salad: Serve warm buttered new potatoes on a bed of tender lettuce with salted cucumbers and a dressing of oil, vinegar, paprika, and a pinch of sugar.

Store-Bought Potato Salad

Buy a container of good store-bought potato salad. Then embellish it:

Deviled Egg and Potato Salad: Combine store-bought potato salad with store-bought egg salad or homemade chopped hard-cooked eggs, and a little fresh dill if you have it. Season and sprinkle with paprika.

Instant Salade Russe: Add a few spoonfuls of cooked frozen mixed vegetables to the potato salad, along with a diced pickle or capers, or both.

Deborah's Fatboy 'Tater Salad: Says Deborah, "It's gotta have meat if it's a Fatboy!" Add a dab or two of spicy brown mustard or buy Creole potato salad with its hit o' horse-radish, then toss in savory, smoked meat such as diced ham or smoked turkey, cooked kielbasa, linguiça, or other sausages, cut into bite-size pieces.

Chunks of Tuna: Toss them into a simple mayonnaise-based potato salad; if it doesn't have chopped celery and green onion, add some!

Salade Tiède
aux Pommes de Terre et aux Lardons

○ ● ○ ◗ ○ ●

Browned nuggets of bacon, tender bites of potato, crunchy bitter greens, and tangy, very tangy, warm dressing. Oh, yes, I forgot: little morsels of pungent blue cheese, too.

Oh, this is totally French bistro fare at its best. Make some now—as a first course for dinner, a meal in a bowl for supper, or a salad-y lunch.

◇ Serves 4

12 ounces kidney-shaped new potatoes, such as Pink Fir Apple or Jersey Royals

1 head frisée lettuce, cut into bite-size pieces

2 tablespoons chopped chives, or 1 green onion, thinly sliced

3 to 4 ounces blue cheese, such as Roquefort, aged Gorgonzola, Point Reyes Original Blue, Danish Blue, Cabrales, or whatever your favorite blue cheese is, cut into small half-bite morsels

2 tablespoons extra-virgin olive oil

1 tablespoon mild German or Dijon mustard

2 to 3 tablespoons white wine vinegar

1 tablespoon chopped fresh tarragon, or 1/2 teaspoon dried

7 ounces very lean lardons (diced bacon)

Salt and freshly ground black pepper

1 Parboil the potatoes for about 10 minutes, or until almost cooked through. Drain, remove from the heat, and set aside.

2 Arrange the frisée on a big platter. Sprinkle with the chives, blue cheese of choice, and half the olive oil.

3 Mix the mustard with the vinegar and tarragon; set aside.

4 When the potatoes are cool enough to handle, rub the peels off if desired, then cut the potatoes into 1/4-or-so-inch slices.

5 Heat the remaining olive oil in a large, nonstick heavy skillet over medium-high heat. Add the lardons and let them brown in places, then push to the side and add the potatoes. Let the potatoes brown over medium-high heat, turning once or twice for even browning.

6 Meanwhile, drizzle half the mustard vinegar over the salad.

7 Push the bacon and potatoes to one side of the pan, and add the remaining mustard vinegar. Cook over high heat until the liquid reduces, turning the bacon and potatoes once or twice.

8 Pour the bacon and potatoes with the bit of dressing at the bottom of the pan over the salad. Sprinkle with salt and pepper to taste, and serve immediately.

Bruce's Deli Potato Salad

Quintessentially deli potato salad: chunks of creamy potato, crunchy bites of celery, sweet little nubbins of red bell pepper, all creamy-tangy with mayonnaise and yellow mustard, unashamedly zesty with pickle relish. Bruce Blackman makes this potato salad at his deli—Sam's Deli, though the Sam in question is long gone—in the Sunrise area of Sacramento, on the outskirts of the Sierra Foothills. I just love this potato salad. Go ahead and have a bite—I dare you to stop eating it!

◇ Serves 4

1 pound waxy potatoes with good earthy flavor, whole and unpeeled

3 stalks celery, finely chopped

1 onion, finely chopped

¼ red bell pepper, finely chopped

5 to 6 heaping tablespoons mayonnaise

4 to 5 tablespoons yellow mustard

4 tablespoons pickle relish

Salt and pepper

1 Cook the potatoes in gently boiling water until just tender. Drain and let cool.

2 Combine the celery with the onion and bell pepper.

3 When the potatoes are cool enough to handle, peel and cut into bite-size morsels. Toss in the mayonnaise, then add the mustard and the pickle relish to taste.

4 Fold in the celery, onion, and bell pepper, and season to taste with salt and pepper. Chill until ready to serve.

Old Country Potato Salad
with Dill and Purslane

This potato salad really is from Russia, shared with me a number of years ago by a Soviet émigré. Purslane—a unique leafy green of the succulent family, which can be either domestic or wild— gives a tangy, fresh burst of flavor to this rich, dill-seasoned potato salad. Adjust the amounts of everything to taste—for a creamier dressing, add more mayonnaise or yogurt; for more zest, add extra capers; and so forth. Find the fresh-tasting purslane at farmers' markets or Turkish grocers, or hunt for it in your own backyard or city streets. If you cannot find it, add a handful of arugula leaves or watercress instead.

◇ Serves 4

12 ounces whole, smallish waxy potatoes, such as fingerlings

3 to 4 tablespoons mayonnaise

3 to 4 tablespoons Greek or other thick yogurt, *laban*, or sour cream, stirred until smooth

1 to 2 teaspoons chopped fresh dill

2 to 3 green onions, thinly sliced

1 teaspoon capers, either salt-cured or brined

Juice of 1/4 lemon

Salt and pepper

3/4 to 1 cup purslane leaves, or about 1 1/2 to 2 cups purslane leaves and stems, cut to about 1- to 2-inch lengths

1 Place the potatoes in a saucepan with cold water to cover. Bring to a boil, then reduce the heat, and cook at a bubbling simmer until potatoes are just tender, for 10 to 15 minutes. Drain and set aside to cool.

2 Slice the potatoes thickly, removing as much of the skin as easily comes off, leaving on a little bit for both texture and ease of slicing.

3 Toss the potatoes with the mayonnaise, yogurt, dill, green onions, capers, and lemon juice to taste. Season to taste with salt and pepper.

4 Fold in the purslane and serve.

Causa a la Limono
Peruvian Mashed Potato Salad with Lemon, Olive Oil, Olives, and Chiles

○ ● ○ ◗ ○ ●

Spicy mashed potatoes, lashed with extra-virgin olive oil and lots of lemon, oomphed up with onion and garlic, and zesty pickled vegetables—this is my take on a traditional Peruvian dish, Causa a la Limono. I like it puckery and tangy; I even splash in a bit of the marinade from the olive jar. My buddy Noah Stroe comes from Peru; I once made *causa* with his late mother, and the experience was unforgettable. Her eyes flashed as she described the joys of the dish, she smiled, we laughed, we chopped, she looked elegant. I felt I had been all the way to South America after spending the afternoon with her.

Since the dish itself is bland looking—a creamy expanse of mashed potato—serve it with leafy green lettuce; slices of sweet potatoes; boiled yellow, blue, or red potatoes; roasted red bell pepper; chunks of corn on the cob; black olives; and wedges of mild Jack cheese. Hard-cooked egg halves and pink shrimp could also share the plate.

◇ Serves 4 to 6

3 pounds russet or yellow-fleshed potatoes, peeled and quartered or cut into chunks

1½ pounds onions, finely chopped

3 to 4 garlic cloves, chopped

¼ to ½ cup fresh lemon juice

⅓ to ½ cup extra-virgin olive oil

½ cup sliced pimiento-stuffed green olives, plus a tablespoon or two of the brine

½ to 1 pickled jalapeño chile, chopped, plus ½ to 1 teaspoon of the marinade

A pinch of red pepper flakes, or ½ fresh red chile, chopped

Salt

Garnish: head of butter lettuce; 1 to 2 cooked yellow, blue, or red potatoes, peeled and sliced; 1 small cooked sweet potato or yam, sliced; 1 roasted red bell pepper cut into strands (from a jar is fine); 1 ear of corn, cut into rounds; a handful of Kalamata olives; 4 ounces mild cheese such as Jack, cut into small triangle shapes

1 Cook the potatoes in gently boiling water until tender; drain and mash.

2 Add the chopped onions, garlic, lemon juice, olive oil, green olives, jalapeño, and red pepper flakes. Season to taste with salt.

3 Let cool. To serve, make a bed of the lettuce and mound the *causa* on top, garnished with the yellow, blue, or red potatoes; sweet potato; bell pepper; corn; olives; and cheese.

Chef Arlene Coco's
and Avery Island's Cajun Potato Salad

○ ● ○ ◗ ○ ◗

I owe this salad to Chef Arlene Coco as well as my visit to Avery Island, home to Tabasco sauce.

Arlene is a Cajun girl who now lives in the the cold North. We met in Naples, Italy—shortly after I first visited the bayou, which was shortly before Hurricane Katrina. As we ate our way through delicious Campania, in between plates of pasta pomodoro, we fell into a deep weeklong conversation about Cajun cooking. I had swooned under the spell of New Orleans, and fallen in love with the bayou, having been a guest of the McElhenny family (hot pepper growers and makers of Tabasco sauce). Even if there were alligators lying around nearly everywhere, and bugs the size of 747s flapping around my face, I adored it all: the romantic hanging Spanish moss on Avery Island, the slow gentle pace of everyday life, and the utter warmth and hospitality of the people.

◇ Serves 4 to 6

1½ pounds small, tender new potatoes (creamers)

1 heaping tablespoon sour cream

1 heaping tablespoon mayonnaise

4 green onions, chopped

¼ green bell pepper, chopped

½ teaspoon celery seeds

¼ to ½ teaspoon yellow mustard

1 to 2 teaspoons Worcestershire sauce

1 or 2 hard-cooked eggs, shelled and diced

½ teaspoon horseradish

1 teaspoon spicy brown mustard or mustard seeds

A few drops Tabasco sauce

Salt and pepper

1 Boil the potatoes in their skins until just tender. Pour off the water and set aside. When cool enough to handle, either remove the skins or leave them on (I prefer the latter), then cut them into bite-size pieces, either halves, quarters, or chunks, depending on their size.

2 Transfer the potatoes to a large bowl, and mix in the sour cream, mayonnaise, green onions, bell pepper, celery seeds, yellow mustard, Worcestershire sauce, eggs, horseradish, and brown mustard.

3 Toss well and taste. Add more horseradish or brown mustard if you want. Season to taste with Tabasco and salt and pepper. Chill until ready to serve.

Bollywood Batata Bowl

○ ● ○ ● ○ ●

This dish is a Bollywood version of potato salad: full of pizzazzy flavors and style, but really simple to make. Diced boiled potatoes are served with a drizzle of tamarind chutney (*immli*), a dollop of cilantro-mint yogurt (*raita*), and the crunch of fried chickpea noodles (*sev*), a variation on a Mumbai street food, spiffed up a bit by frying the *poppadums* in the shape of a bowl and serving the salad in that. The combination of tastes and textures is divine. If you don't feel like shaping a bowl from the *poppadums*, use smaller ones and scatter them around the salad, or fry regular big ones and break them up into several-bite shards, then garnish the salad with these.

I've broken the recipe into separate parts. If you don't wish to make the *immli* from scratch, you can use mango chutney instead (see quickie variation on page 76).

◇ Serves 4

Poppadum Bowls

Oil for frying, about 1 inch deep

8 *poppadums*

Immli

3 ounces tamarind, in block form, without seeds

1 cup water

5 dried seedless dates

1 teaspoon cumin

1 tablespoon sugar

Juice of 1/2 lemon or several shakes of vinegar, or a combination

Raita

1 1/2- to 2-inch piece ginger, coarsely chopped

1/2 bunch cilantro, coarsely chopped

1/2 bunch fresh mint, coarsely chopped, or 2 tablespoons dried mint

2 teaspoons sugar

5 to 6 tablespoons low-fat yogurt

Aromatic Salt

1 tablespoon coarse sea salt

1 teaspoon cumin, either ground or seeds

1 teaspoon ground cinnamon

1 teaspoon dried mint

1/2 teaspoon turmeric

1/2 teaspoon ground fenugreek

1/2 teaspoon ground allspice

1 pound medium-size, slightly waxy potatoes

continued

continued

Garnish

2 to 3 tablespoons *sev*, or a Bombay mixture of *sev*, toasted nuts, and legumes, per person

1 onion, finely chopped

1 to 2 fresh chile peppers, red, green, or a combination

5 to 7 tablespoons chopped fresh cilantro

1 to 2 limes, cut into wedges

½ cup plain low-fat yogurt (optional)

Tabasco sauce (optional)

Lime pickle (optional)

1 To make the *poppadum* bowls: Heat the oil in a heavy nonstick skillet over medium-high heat. When the oil is smoking, add a *poppadum*, just one, and let it cook in the hot oil. The oil is the right temperature when the wafer curls and wrinkles right away, and grows light and parchment-like. Do not let it brown too much, they cook very quickly; using tongs, turn it over, let the second side cook until lightly golden and browned, only a few moments, then immediately transfer to a deep cereal bowl and gently press into the bowl so that the *poppadum* takes a bit of the bowl's shape. The *poppadum* will quickly grow brittle; remove and turn upside down to drain it of oil and dry out. Repeat the procedure for each *poppadum*. This can be done up to two days ahead of time and kept in a dry cool place.

2 To make the *immli*: Combine the tamarind, water, and dates in a saucepan and bring to a boil. Reduce the heat and simmer for about 5 minutes, or until the tamarind melts a bit and grows soft. Remove from the heat and let cool. Whirl through a food processor or a blender, and pour through a sieve to be rid of any seeds. Transfer to a bowl, and stir in the cumin, sugar (using more or less if you want), and lemon juice. This can be done up to two days ahead of time and stored in the refrigerator.

3 To make the *raita*: In a food processor combine the ginger, cilantro, and mint. Whirl until it is smooth, then add the sugar to your taste and the yogurt and whirl until it forms a lightly green, flecked mixture. This is best made the day of eating.

4 To make the aromatic salt: Combine the sea salt, cumin, cinnamon, mint, turmeric, fenugreek, and allspice in a bowl. This can be stored for 2 weeks in an airtight jar.

5 Place the potatoes in a saucepan and cover with water. Bring to a boil, then reduce the heat, and cook at a gentle simmer until the potatoes are just tender. Drain and leave to cool, then gently peel the skin away. Just before serving, dice into small pieces and sprinkle with the aromatic salt.

6 Place a *poppadum* bowl on each serving plate, and spoon the potato mixture into it. In each bowl place a handful of *sev*, a sprinkling of onion, chile, and cilantro, then more *sev*. Spoon a big dab of the *immli* on one side, the *raita* on another, and accompany by lime wedges, and plain yogurt if you want, with Tabasco sauce or lime pickle on the side for those who dare.

Variation:

Quickie Version—Potatoes with Sev and Chutney

When you want a hit of Indian street flavor but are short on time and effort, you can make this quickie version. Dice one or two cold, peeled boiled potatoes per person. Toss with chopped onion and chopped cilantro as desired, about a tablespoon of each per person. Serve with a dab of mango chutney, a dollop of yogurt, a handful of *sev* or a Bombay mixture of *sev*, toasted nuts, and legumes, scattered over the top.

Salade Russe

Russian Potato Salad with Beets, Chopped Pickle, and Fresh Dill

○ ● ○ ● ○ ●

Salad Russe is one of the world's most famous salads. English countryside? Russian salad. Russia? Salade Russe. Go to Egypt, you'll find Salade Russe, as you will find it in Poland. Malaysia? Salade Russe. A good Salade Russe is simply the best potato salad ever, a creamy mixture with lots of lovely extras: diced vegetables, pungent pickley things, and in this case, diced beets, which give it a pink hue. Salade Russe is especially good with herring, smoked fish, thinly sliced cold cuts; delicious with vodka, for lunch or *zakuski* (appetizers).

In Europe, beets can be purchased already cooked; sometimes in the United States I find these vacuum packed and ready to be stored on the shelf. If unavailable, cook your own ahead of time either by boiling or steaming, whole and unpeeled. Beet skins slip off when cooked; if you try to peel them beforehand, they lose color and goodness. Beets may also be roasted: Place in a baking dish in a single layer along with a chopped onion or two, a few garlic cloves, a sprinkling of sugar, a shaking of red wine vinegar, and cover tightly. Bake for about an hour, or until the beets are tender.

◇ Serves 4

2 roasted or boiled beets, cooled, peeled, and diced

4 medium-size boiled potatoes (12 to 14 ounces), cooled, peeled, and diced

¼ onion, finely chopped

2 to 3 tablespoons sour cream

1 medium dill pickle, diced

½ tangy, juicy apple, finely diced

A shake or two of red wine vinegar

Salt

½ teaspoon sugar

½ to 1 teaspoon mustard seeds

1 tablespoon chopped fresh dill

1 Combine the beets and potatoes with the onion, sour cream, pickle, and apple. Season to taste with the vinegar, salt, sugar, and mustard seeds.

2 Chill until ready to serve, then sprinkle with the dill.

Variation:
Another Russian Salad

Instead of beets, sometimes I add about ½ cup cooked peas and diced cooked carrots to the mixture. Yum.

Boiled, Stewed

& Saucy Sides

5

chapter

Boiled potatoes are delicious freshly cooked. Leftover the next day, they are like a cache of culinary jewels—ready to be turned into salads, hash, or hash browns, or cut up into a variety of dishes.

For boiling, use waxy potatoes; they keep their shape and have a better texture for boiling. Place the potatoes in a saucepan with cold water to cover, and bring to a boil over medium-high heat. Once boiling, reduce the heat to a rolling, bubbling simmer, cover, and cook for a further 10 minutes or so, depending on the size and age of your potatoes or potato chunks. Small potatoes or potatoes cut into chunks may cook in as little as 10 minutes; large potatoes could take 30 minutes or even longer.

You can cook potatoes in their skins, which I think gives a more earthy flavor, or you can peel them before you cook them. Once cooked, the skin comes off quite easily, using a paring knife and your fingers, so this is another option.

Though I prefer plain water, or water with a big pinch of salt added, my husband, who grew up with Scottish parents, swears that a pinch of sugar brings out the potatoey-ness of the tuber. And the late legendary food writer Richard Olney preferred boiling potatoes in water to which some herbs—such as bay leaf, thyme, rosemary, parsley—garlic cloves, and chunks of onion have been added. This almost broth will perfume your potatoes with the flavors of the French countryside.

To tell if potatoes are done, pierce them with a sharp knife, skewer, or fork tines. If they are tender and the knife pierces them, then the potatoes are ready. If the knife stops in its tracks, the potato needs to cook awhile longer. Avoid piercing the potatoes over and over, as the water leaches into the potato and turns the tuber watery in flavor and texture. An easy way to tell if the potatoes are done is this: Skewer one or two of the potatoes or potato chunks with a bamboo skewer. When potatoes are cooked through, the skewer will come right out. If the skewer still has a bit of sticking and won't slide out easily, the potato's not quite ready yet.

Once the potatoes are cooked through, drain the water and return the potatoes to the stove for a few moments to dry out. Cook, covered, over medium-low heat for a few minutes, taking care that you do not burn the potatoes. Shake every so often, to rid them of their wateriness. To serve the potatoes whole, a sprinkle of salt tossed over the boiled potatoes before you dry them over the heat is recommended. It makes the potatoes taste almost as if they have been cooked in the sea. I prefer salting the potatoes like this rather than cooking the potatoes in salted water, as there is a very subtle sweet-earthy-salty contrast.

Simple Dishes
with Warm Boiled Potatoes

- Serve warm boiled new potatoes with hard-cooked egg and a handful of arugula. Dress with a cruet of extra-virgin olive oil, a wedge of lemon to squeeze on, and a sprinkling of coarse sea salt.

- Cook sliced yellow crookneck squash with chunks or slices of potato; when they are just tender, serve them in a bowl topped with a pat of butter, a sprinkling of salt, and chopped fresh dill.

- Serve freshly boiled warm potatoes broken up with a fork and topped with thinly sliced green onions, butter, and Greek yogurt or sour cream.

- Sprinkle quartered potatoes with the Middle Eastern spice za'atar, a handful of greens such as arugula, purslane, or watercress, and a dollop of Greek yogurt.

- Scatter chunks of warm boiled potatoes with capers, chopped parsley, and extra-virgin olive oil, and serve lemon wedges on the side.

- Combine 1/4 cup Greek yogurt or Middle Eastern laban with 1 tablespoon grated fresh ginger, the juice and zest of 1/2 lemon, 1 teaspoon soy sauce, a few drops of sesame oil, plus salt to taste. Stir in 2 to 3 thinly sliced green onions. Spoon this east-west-flavored sauce over boiled fingerlings or tiny Yukon nuggets—or any small potato, really.

- Serve the boiled blue-fleshed potatoes, cooked and shredded coarsely, in a light little pile in a ceramic spoon. Sprinkle with tangy-hot sauce chien: 1 tablespoon each lime juice and vinegar, a grating of lime zest, and a few big glugs of hot pepper sauce such as siracha, plus salt to taste.

Two Marvelous Potato Dishes from Campania

- **Anna Maria Mennella's Bitter Greens with Potatoes from her and her husband Antonio's olive farm, Madonna dell'Olivo, in the Salerno countryside:** Warm 4 to 6 thinly sliced or coarsely chopped cloves of garlic in 2 or 3 tablespoons olive oil, then add a large, cored head of escarole, cut up into bite-size lengths. Cover and braise slowly, 30 to 40 minutes, adding a few spoonfuls of water if needed. Salt and pepper to taste. Meanwhile, boil about 8 ounces—3 medium—waxy peeled potatoes until tender. Drain, and break with a fork into uneven crumbles and chunks. Toss with greens over low heat, then serve together at room temperature with an added drizzle of olive oil. (I recently served leftovers hot, and topped with melting Emmentaler cheese. Mmmmm, delish.)

- **Gorgeous Napoletana Sonia Carbone's Old-Fashioned Potatoes and Peppers from the streets of Napoli and the Campania countryside:** Boil a pound of peeled, creamy small waxy potatoes and keep warm. When they are cooked, lightly sauté 6 to 7 cloves thinly sliced or coarsely chopped garlic in 3 to 4 tablespoons extra-virgin olive oil, then add 5 to 6 pickled cherry peppers, cut into thin strips or chopped coarsely. Coarsely break up the potatoes with a fork, and pour over the sizzling hot peppers. Serve right away, hot or at room temperature. "Delicious with grilled steak or other meats," says Sonia, her eyes flashing with delight at just the thought of this recipe's tastiness. (If cherry peppers are not available, use a combination of roasted red peppers and green pickled Italian or Greek peppers. You can use either sweet or mildly spicy peppers.)

Raclette

○ ● ○ ◐ ○ ◖

When I mention a book on potatoes, nine people out of ten will ask, hopefully, "Raclette?"
What is it about raclette that is so enticing? I mean, it's a simple dish: sizzling melty cheese, hot boiled
potatoes, marinated or pickled onions, or both, as in this recipe. No cooking skills or acrobatics
required. But perhaps that is it exactly. Raclette is all about the potatoes, and the cheese. And the
temperature: you must keep the cheese hot, and the potatoes pretty warm, too, or the cheese seizes up
unappealingly. For perfection in the temperature and organizational department, there are special
machines to melt the edges of the cheese, so that each little plate of raclette can be tempting from start to
finish, and you can then progress to another plate of the deliciousness. Lacking a special machine,
I line up little baking pans and warm a stack of little plates.

Raclette, by the way, is the name of the French and Swiss mountain cheeses the dish is based on;
they are similar but by no means the same—taste both and decide which is your favorite. I quite often
make raclette using whichever cheese I happen to have in the house; recently I made a mixture of young
(twelve months) Grana Padano and Jack, sprinkled with white wine, and it was terrific.

◇ Serves 4 to 6

Marinated Onions

2 red onions, sliced thinly crosswise

2 tablespoons sugar

6 tablespoons red or white wine vinegar

Raclette

2 to 2½ pounds small tender new potatoes

1 pound French or Swiss raclette cheese, or a mixture of other cheeses (see headnote), thinly sliced

1 to 2 tablespoons dry white wine

Small cornichons, or dill pickles, sliced

Pickled onions, preferably the large-ish malt vinegar pickled English onions, cut into quarters

continued

continued

1 To make the marinated onions: Place the sliced red onions in a bowl and pour boiling water over them, to cover. Leave for about thirty minutes, to soften in both texture and flavor.

2 Drain, then combine with the sugar and vinegar. Set aside. This can be made four or five days ahead and kept in the refrigerator.

3 To make the raclette: Cook the potatoes in gently boiling salted water until they are just tender, but not overcooked. Drain, then return to the pot; cover and keep them hot.

4 Divide the cheese into three batches and arrange in three pans. Sprinkle the cheese with the wine.

5 Arrange the marinated onions in a bowl and place on the table, along with the cornichons and pickled onions.

6 Heat the broiler, and warm small plates (preferably one per person for each batch of raclette so that the dish can be eaten piping hot) in the oven. When ready to go, place several hot potatoes onto the first batch of hot plates.

7 Place the first pan of cheese under the broiler. Heat, watching the cheese all the while so that it doesn't burn, until it melts and sizzles; remove immediately and divide the cheese into individual portions onto each hot plate of potatoes. Whisk immediately to the table, so that the potatoes can be eaten hot, with the pickles.

8 When the first round of potatoes and cheese is finished, gather up the plates and repeat. Three rounds of potatoes and cheese should please even the most passionate of cheese-and-potato-holics.

Kartoffel mit Frankfurter Gruen Sosse

Hot Buttered Potatoes with Frankfurt Green Sauce

○ ● ○ ● ○ ●

Gruen Sosse, or green sauce from Frankfurt, Germany, is a thick, creamy mixture of as many herbs as you can find, bound together with chopped hard-cooked egg, sour cream, yogurt, and seasonings. It's like the best party dip you could imagine, and it's eaten on nearly everything: sold in delis, dabbed onto a plate in a traditional restaurant, dolloped onto plates in homes. I've even eaten the creamy green sauce blanketing two fried potato pancakes at the Konstablerwache marketplace. The marketplace looked and felt like a Brueghel painting, and there were potatoes everywhere—piles of home fries, towers of potato pancakes, gleaming globes of creamy-colored boiled potatoes.

This recipe is an adaptation of Rebecca Hecht's, who lives in Frankfurt and has become adept at whipping up Gruen Sosse. Her friend and mine, ballet choreographer Noah Gelber, often told me about how good her version is, and how I *had* to taste it. One bite and I thought, this is the nirvana of green sauces. Rebecca tells me that a typical Frankfurter Gruen Sosse consists of seven different seasonal herbs and follows the season throughout the year. In spring they include parsley, sorrel, chervil, burnet, lemon balm, borage, chives, and watercress, while later in the season basil might make its fragrant appearance. Along with the potatoes it's served on—young, old, tender, mealy—the herby sauce truly changes with the calendar.

I like the combination of herbs and greenery included here; serve with boiled new potatoes, a handful of watercress, and a gently hard-cooked egg per person.

◇ Serves 4

Frankfurter Gruen Sosse

4 eggs

1 ounce fresh spinach leaves, or about 6 tablespoons frozen spinach (you want to end up with cooked, chopped, and squeezed-dry spinach)

4 to 6 green onions, thinly sliced

2 tablespoons chopped fresh parsley

3 tablespoons chopped watercress or arugula leaves

1½ tablespoons chopped fresh tarragon

2 to 3 teaspoons chopped dill

½ cup sour cream

⅓ cup yogurt

1 tablespoon extra-virgin olive oil

1 to 2 teaspoons white wine vinegar

½ teaspoon mild Dijon or German mustard

Small pinch sugar

Salt and pepper

1 pound tiny baby waxy potatoes such as La Rattes, fingerlings, Pink Fir Apple, or assorted potatoes, unpeeled

Unsalted butter, for buttering potatoes

1 To make the Frankfurter Gruen Sosse: Hard boil the eggs, and run them under cold water for a few minutes. When cool enough to handle, peel and coarsely chop. Set aside.

2 Cook the spinach leaves in a little water until wilted and darkened; remove from the hot water and set aside. When cool enough to handle, squeeze dry and finely chop.

3 Combine the egg, spinach, green onions, parsley, watercress, tarragon, and dill in a food processor and whirl to purée.

4 Transfer this finely ground green herby mixture to a bowl, add the sour cream and yogurt to taste, and stir well, then add the olive oil, vinegar, mustard, and sugar. Season to taste with salt and pepper, and stir together well.

5 Chill at least a half hour before serving; several hours is even better.

6 Cook the potatoes in gently boiling water until they are tender. Drain and place in a bowl.

7 Let your guests serve themselves, open up the little potatoes, dab them with a nubbin of butter to melt in, and then top each with a spoonful of the green herby sauce.

Papas Chorreadas
Potatoes with Spicy, Tomatoey Cheese Sauce

○ ● ○ ◗ ○ ◗

Chorreadas is eaten spooned onto potatoes and almost anything else in Colombia. Naturally, potatoes are a Number One ingredient for being blanketed with the luscious tomatoey cheese sauce—it's not a million miles away from Peru, the home of the potato, where a similar dish, Papas a la Huancaina, is traditional. *Chorreadas* is spicier and full of tomatoes, while *huancaina* is made with the Peruvian chile, *aji* (or amarillo, limon, colorado, whichever you find), which has a citrusy flavor to go with its Andean heat.

Traditionally, of course, local cheese would be used; I use a combination of different cheeses— for instance, a little feta for salty milky flavor, a little Wensleydale or Jack for a mild curd, and some Cheddar because it's so deliciously melty. To finish it off, some fermented milk such as sour cream or Greek yogurt—I'm not claiming authenticity here, just deliciousness.

Leftover *chorreadas* is luscious; serve it wrapped in a soft corn tortilla, or melted on top of a burger. I've been known to eat the leftovers with a spoon for breakfast.

Use potatoes of different colors if you like, and I find that a garnish of corn kernels is delish and also looks very nice.

I specify red jalapeño chiles, which are easy to find, but for true Andean flavor, use *aji* chiles; if fresh are not available, use puréed *aji* from a jar. If you choose to use *aji*, add a little chopped red pepper for freshness and color.

continued

continued

◇ Serves 4 to 6

12 to 16 small new potatoes, about three per person (choose different colors, if possible), unpeeled

1/2 cup corn kernels, either fresh or frozen

2 tablespoons olive oil

2 onions, chopped

3 garlic cloves, chopped

1 to 2 mild red jalapeño or *aji* chiles, chopped (more if you like, or if these are particularly mild)

1 1/2 teaspoons turmeric

1 teaspoon cumin

1/4 teaspoon ground ginger

2 cups diced tomatoes (canned is fine; include the juices)

1/4 cup chopped cilantro

1 1/2 cups mixed cheeses, about 1/2 cup each crumbled feta, diced Jack or Hispanic Panela, and shredded Cheddar

1 cup sour cream, or Greek yogurt

1 Cook the potatoes in a heavy saucepan with water to cover. Boil gently until they are just tender; do not overcook. This should take about 15 minutes. Drain; using a clean cloth, hold each potato and, with a sharp paring knife, peel off the skin. Return to the pot, cover, and keep warm.

2 In a separate saucepan, with water to cover, bring corn kernels to a boil, then remove from the heat. Drain and keep warm. Fresh young corn needs only the quickest cooking to retain its fresh, sweet quality.

3 In a heavy nonstick skillet, heat the olive oil over medium-low heat, and lightly sauté the onions with the garlic and chiles until they are softened, for about 7 minutes.

4 Sprinkle in the turmeric, cumin, and ginger, stir around to cook the spices for only a moment or two, then add the tomatoes and cilantro and cook over medium-low heat until most of the liquid has evaporated, for about 10 minutes.

5 Stir in the cheeses and sour cream, and slowly heat together, stirring, until it forms a cheesy, creamy mixture.

6 Slice the potatoes and arrange on a plate or platter, with the sauce alongside it and a sprinkling of corn kernels.

Yellow-Fleshed Potatoes
with Asparagus, Duck or Goose Fat, and Truffle Paste

○ ● ○ ● ○ ●

Dilemma: This dish looks nicest with the truffle paste dabbed on the plate alongside. Tossed with the truffle paste, it looks a bit sludgey and gray, but tastes fab. It has to be your choice here. You can use any type of truffle paste or condiment with this. I used summer truffle paste in testing the recipe; black truffle paste mixed with asparagus purée, white truffle paste, or a smooth concoction of black truffle with porcini would be divine, too. Note about truffle paste: While it often comes in a jar, tubes keep it fresher for longer. And, you can always satisfy temptation with a little squirt into the mouth each time you walk past the fridge.

◇ Serves 4

12 to 16 ounces yellow-fleshed potatoes, such as Yukon Gold or Mayan Gold, whole with skins on

1 smallish bunch asparagus, trimmed, the pieces cut into bite-size lengths

4 to 6 tablespoons goose or duck fat

2 to 3 garlic cloves, chopped

4 tablespoons truffle paste (see headnote)

Salt and pepper

1 Cook the potatoes in water to cover over medium-high heat until they are just tender.

2 Add the asparagus and continue cooking for about 5 minutes, or until it is just tender and the potatoes are very tender. Remove from the heat and drain. Set aside until the potatoes are just warm enough to handle for peeling.

3 Hold on to the potatoes with a cloth so that you do not burn your hand; peel the potatoes using a paring knife to help grab and dislodge the skin. Break up the potatoes into large chunks; smaller ones will form on their own as you break the potatoes with your fork.

4 In a heavy skillet, warm the fat. Do not heat it to smoking, just gently warm it.

5 Toss the potato bits and asparagus into the warming fat. Sprinkle with the garlic, then dot with the truffle paste. Gently toss together with a spatula, taking care not to mash or overmix the potatoes. Season to taste with salt and pepper.

6 Turn the potatoes onto a plate and serve right away.

Aloo Tamatar Bhaji
Gingered Tomato-Curry Potatoes

○ ● ◇ ◑ ○ ●

These potatoes are full of rambunctious spice and tangy tomato, golden
with turmeric, and fragrant with garlic and ginger. Breaking the potatoes rather than
mashing or slicing gives a delight of texture. The variety of sizes means that each piece of potato has
absorbed differing amounts of flavor, making each bite unique. It's all about variety, that spice of life.
The potatoes are good hot, but they are also good cold. Like Goldilocks,
I find hot is simply too hot and cold is that wee bit too cold; room temperature is just right.

◇ Serves 4

**1 pound small new potatoes, such as Jersey Royals,
Pink Fir Apples, or creamers**

1/2 teaspoon turmeric

**Several large pinches sea salt, preferably coarse grain
or flaked**

5 to 6 tablespoons extra-virgin olive oil

1 1/2 tablespoons chopped fresh ginger

6 to 8 garlic cloves, chopped

2 shallots, peeled and chopped

2 teaspoons yellow or black mustard seeds

1/2 teaspoon whole cumin seeds

Large pinch of ground coriander

Pinch of asafetida

Medium to large pinch of red pepper flakes

**4 to 6 large ripe tomatoes, grated over the large holes
of a box grater**

Pinch of ground cumin

3 tablespoons chopped cilantro

1 Boil the potatoes in their skins until they are just tender; drain
and set aside. When cool enough to handle, hold on to each
with a clean towel and peel, then break the potatoes up coarsely
with a fork, each potato into 3 or so pieces; remove any extra
skin that can be picked out, and toss the broken potatoes with
the turmeric, using a little more than called for in the recipe, if
needed, to turn the potatoes a golden yellow. Season to taste
with salt.

2 In a nonstick skillet, heat the olive oil over medium-high
heat. Add the ginger, garlic, shallots, and mustard seeds. Cook

continued

continued

until the mustard seeds start to pop a little, then sprinkle in the cumin seeds, coriander, asafetida, and red pepper flakes.

3 Add the tomato, and cook mixture over medium heat until it makes a sauce, then gently add the potatoes, and toss them in the tomato mixture until well combined.

4 Continue to cook down until the tomatoes turn into a thick sauce that clings to the potatoes. Season to taste with salt and sprinkle with ground cumin.

5 Serve warm, or at room temperature, sprinkled with the chopped cilantro.

Variation:
Aloo Methi

Methi is fresh fenugreek leaves; you can purchase them at a farmers' market or an Indian, Bangladeshi, or Pakistani grocery shop. To make *aloo methi,* add a bunch of *methi* leaves, coarsely chopped, to the cooking potatoes after you have combined the potatoes with the tomato mixture, and cook for about 15 minutes.

Creamy Swedish Potatoes

So there I was, at a smorgasbord somewhere near Orebro, Sweden, in the middle of a snowstorm, in a farmhouse inn next to a frozen lake. There was *wasabrod*—the crisp rye flatbread so beloved by the Scandinavians—and cucumber salad, as well as herrings and smoked salmon, and a savory meatball-like patty in warm, oh-so-meaty gravy. And there in a big crystal bowl was a mass of aromatic, warm diced potatoes awash in a creamy sauce and topped with chives and melting butter. How many times did I revisit the table and that bowl? Don't even ask.

◇ Serves 4 as a side dish

1½ pounds large, white, thin-skinned potatoes, waxy rather than floury, peeled and cut into large-ish dice

1 to 1½ cups heavy (whipping) cream

Salt and black pepper

1 to 2 tablespoons unsalted butter, cut into small pieces

1 bunch chives, thinly sliced

1 Place the potatoes in a saucepan with water to cover. Bring to a boil, then reduce heat to medium, and cook the potatoes on a simmer or low boil, until they are just tender. Do not let them overcook or become mushy; cooking time should be about 10 minutes.

2 Drain, then combine the hot potatoes with the cream in the saucepan and return to the heat. Cook over medium or medium-high heat, letting the cream evaporate and the potatoes absorb quite a bit of its richness. Do not stir; rather, turn the potatoes gently once or twice using a spatula. If you stir them, you will have mashed potatoes.

3 When the cream is thickened and mostly evaporated, season to taste with salt and pepper, then gently tip the mixture into the serving bowl. Dot the top with butter (which will melt all over the top and run here and there in delicious rivulets) and sprinkle with chives. Serve right away.

chapter

Mashed potatoes, smooshy, starchy, creamy, are possibly the most irresistible of foods for almost any age. Babies love mashed potatoes, predictably, delightful to either spoon up or simply push into their mouths with pudgy hands, sitting happily in their highchairs. Children love mashed potatoes, the creamy, bland, soft deliciousness, to eat alongside meat or fish, or to make into a polka-dot pattern by arranging their peas, just so, in the potatoes. Almost all adults love mashed potatoes, either because it makes them feel as happy as a child, or because they are eating a very, very indulgent version. And when you reach your golden years, mashed potatoes are there, waiting for you, nothing too hard to chew, nothing too challenging on the palate. Though, to be honest, today's mashed potatoes are nothing like yesterday's mashed potatoes. Today's mashed potatoes are superstars, not satisfied to sit on the side next to the main course, bland and getting their personality from the gravy or sauce alongside. No, today's mashed potatoes go wild, fluffed with garlic, or melty cheese, or tomatoey sauces, or pungent herbs. Almost anything is delish in mashed potatoes. And once, I was treated to a buffet of mashed potatoes in a posh trendy restaurant.

For delicious, perfect-for-you mash, choose the right potatoes. Smooth, silky mashed potatoes need floury potatoes; nutty, chunky crushed potatoes call for waxy spuds.

Mashed and Crushed,

on Your Plate or in a Bowl

Leftover Mashed Potatoes

If you have leftovers, here is a list of things to make.

Filling for Tunisian Brik Pastries: Lay out a length of phyllo pastry, at one corner place a tablespoon of mashed potato with an indentation, then plop a raw egg into the indentation. Sprinkle with capers and shredded cheese, then fold over and over again enclosing the egg completely. Fry in several inches of hot oil on each side until the pastry turns golden, then remove and place on a baking sheet. Bake at 400°F for about 5 minutes or until the pastry crisps and turns golden brown and the egg inside is poached, that is the white is firm, the yolk is runny. Serve with a dip of hot harissa sauce from a tube mixed with water. Or make your own: Mix 1 tablespoon paprika, a few shakes of cayenne pepper, a squeeze of lemon juice, a pinch of cumin, and enough water to make a thin sauce, and warm through until it just boils.

Meatballs and Meat Loaf: Add leftover mashed potatoes to ground meat for meatballs or meat loaf, along with a handful of bread crumbs and a shower of Parmesan cheese. Blanket with savory tomato sauce.

Shepherd's Pie: Use leftover mash as the topping on a shepherd's pie of browned ground lamb, a cottage pie of browned ground beef, or a fish pie of chunks of fish and seafood in a light brothy cream.

Shortcut Pierogi: Make a filling of mashed potatoes mixed with lots of fried onions and bound together with beaten egg. Use wonton wrappers or Japanese *gyoza* wrappers to fold over and enclose this filling. Cook by boiling or by pan-browning, then adding a little bit of water, pot sticker–style. Serve with melted butter, thinly sliced green onions, or fried sliced yellow onion. I like a few drops of vinegar as well.

Soup: Use a few spoonfuls to thicken a creamy soup.

Trish's Potato Patties: My buddy Trish Kelly grew up in a big Italian-Irish family, in which potatoes figured prominently. If I ask Trish what she's doing for dinner on any given day, she'll probably mention the potatoes first. Here is one from her table: To 1 to 2 cups leftover mashed potatoes, add about 1/2 cup freshly grated Parmesan, Grana Padano, or pecorino, as well as 2 tablespoons flour, and 1 egg plus 1 egg white, lightly beaten together. Form into patties or pancake-like shapes, and dredge with bread crumbs, then brown in a small amount of olive oil in a hot heavy nonstick skillet.

Yapingachos: Add a few heaping spoonfuls of cottage cheese and Parmesan to a bowl of leftover mashed potatoes, along with a beaten egg, a thinly sliced green onion or two, and a spoonful or two of flour. Form into patties, dip into beaten egg, dredge in crumbs, and brown in olive oil or butter.

Bangers and Mash

Bangers and mash is the quintessential British comfort food. While I grew up eating sauerkraut with hot dogs, and sautéed peppers with Italian sausage, and black beans with chorizo or spicy sausage, and *merguez* with *frites*, the British eat a big pile of mashed potatoes with a sausage or two strewn around the plate. While once the mash could be only plain, now with the influence of spices and global ingredients, bangers and mash just might have a whiff of garlic and a collection of different types of sausages. And gravy? Definitely gravy. Kick off your shoes, pour yourself a nice glass of beer—warm, please—and eat your bangers and mash with a spoon.

Rather than one definitive dish, I'm allowing you to create your own. First, choose your favorite mashed potato recipe and prepare it. Then, choose a sausage that sounds like a good match. I like to mix and match sometimes, preparing a selection of sausages so that each person can have a slice or two of different ones. Brown the sausages until they are cooked through; cooking time will depend on the type of sausage you have chosen.

Some suggested pairings:

- **Thai curry chicken sausages Green Thai Curry Mash (variation, page 100)**
- **Yucatecan sausages with Mexican Mash from Highgrove (page 106)**
- **Toulouse sausages with Crazy Rich, Creamy Double-Garlic Mashed Potatoes (page 101)**
- **Duck and green peppercorn sausages, with red wine pan juices, with Irresistible Basil Mashed Potatoes (page 105)**
- **Irish sausages, or Spanish chorizo sausages, with Colcannon (variation, page 100)**

Think about a gravy. If a gravy is desired, remove the sausages from the pan and keep warm. Sauté a thinly sliced onion in the sausage pan until softened and lightly browned, and add a cup of broth such as beef or vegetable, and a cup of wine. Boil it down until it reduces by more than half. Serve alongside the sausages and mash, so that people can spoon a little of this reduced sausage and onion jus over the potatoes.

Great Mashed Potatoes

○ ● ○ ◗ ○ ●

For fluffy, light mashed potatoes, use floury potatoes; for crushed potatoes, in which you
wish to retain firmer chunks, use waxy potatoes.
For the fluffiest potatoes, use a ricer; for a bit more of a sturdy mash, wield that potato masher;
for crushed potatoes, use a fork and only mash and crush here and there. All agree that potatoes must
never be whipped in a food processor or you risk a gluey mess, as the whirling blade breaks
down the walls of the cells, setting free the sticky starch. The amount of milk or cream, and butter,
is purely according to your tastes and desire; add and taste as you go along.

◇ Serves 6

3 pounds potatoes, either floury or waxy (see headnote)

Salt

**1/3 to 1/2 cup hot milk or cream, or as desired for
your preferred consistency**

3 to 5 tablespoons butter

Pepper

1 Peel and cut the potatoes into chunks; place in a saucepan
with cold water to cover, shake in a little salt, and bring to
a boil. Reduce the heat to low and cook until the potatoes are
just tender. (Some cooks prefer boiling the whole potato,
unpeeled, for an earthier flavor, then peeling them—or not—
once tender.)

2 Pour the water off and return the potatoes to the heat for a
few minutes, shaking the pan to evaporate the water and keep
the potatoes light and dry. Cover and set aside, keeping warm.

3 Heat the milk in a saucepan until bubbles form around
the edge.

4 Mash the drained potatoes using your preferred tool—ricer,
masher, or fork—then with a wooden spoon, beat in the hot
milk and butter. Season to taste with salt and pepper.

continued

continued

Variations

Hold the Potatoes, Chef

To hold potatoes, modern chefs have developed this trick: Rice the potatoes with the butter rather than mashing them together. Put them through the ricer a second or even a third time, for maximum fluffiness. Set the pan aside, covered, for up to 2 hours. A few minutes before you are ready to eat, heat the milk in a saucepan and add the buttered mash, in the amount you wish, until you get the right fluffy, creamy consistency.

Champ

Add a bunch of thinly sliced green onions to the milk and then heat through. Stir into your potatoes for a mash that is fragrant and oniony, flecked with green, and ecstasy to eat. In each bowl place a big pat of butter to melt in; use more butter than you think you'd like, more than you know is good for you. Close your eyes and smile your inner potato-eating smile.

Neeps and Tatties

This Scottish dish is also known as *clapshot*—it is a chunky mash of rutabaga (hence the name *neeps*, a Scottish nickname for rutabagas, which are known as turnips in Scotland and *swedes* in England) and potatoes (affectionately nicknamed *tatties* in Scotland). Some say that Neeps and Tatties originated in the Orkney Islands; all agree that it makes the finest, most classic accompaniment to a Burns Night haggis. To prepare Neeps and Tatties: In place of half the potatoes, use an equal amount of peeled, diced rutabaga. Cook and mash as directed, and mix in hot milk, butter, salt and pepper to taste, and chopped chives, if desired.

Green Thai Curry Mash

Mash potatoes as directed, but omit the milk. Add about 4 tablespoons Greek yogurt instead, along with green Thai curry paste (from a jar) to taste—I'd suggest about 2 to 3 teaspoons, or more, depending on how hot it is—and a grating of block coconut cream (or several tablespoons unsweetened liquid coconut cream). Squirt in the juice of a half or whole lime, and serve.

Wasabi-Pea and Potato Mash

With a mortar and pestle, crush a big handful of hot wasabi peas until they form a rough meal. Proceed with the mashed potatoes as directed, mixing in the milk, but omitting the butter. Add the crushed wasabi peas and serve with a drizzle of sesame oil.

Colcannon

Decrease the amount of potatoes to 2 pounds and add a big bunch of kale, cut into strips or coarsely chopped, to the pot of potatoes and cook together. Mash as for champ, with the green onion–infused milk.

Lobster Mash

Make it rich with cream and either a crumble of fish bouillon cube or a few spoonfuls of fish/seafood broth and top it with a nugget of soft lobster butter (diced cooked lobster, with an equal amount of soft butter, and a sprinkling of chopped chives and fresh tarragon to taste). Serve with anything seafoody, such as crisp roasted fish, or with rare grilled steak.

Crazy Rich, Creamy Double-Garlic
Mashed Potatoes

○ ● ○ ● ○ ●

Garlic mashed potatoes: two delicious foods, one blissful bowl. Use milk or cream,
use crème fraîche or don't, cook your garlic cloves along with the potatoes or add chopped
raw garlic at the end—or, follow in the footsteps of the Garlic Queen (me) and do both.
I tend to use more liquid rather than less, as the softer smooth and silky texture is always so much
more pleasurable than a dense potato mash. If you add a little too much milk or cream,
just heat the mixture on the stove over medium or low heat for a few minutes, taking care
that the liquid evaporates but that the potatoes don't burn.

◇ Serves 4 to 6

2 pounds mealy potatoes such as russets, or other baking potatoes, peeled and cut into large chunks (4 to 6 chunks per potato)

8 garlic cloves; 5 whole and peeled, 3 chopped (optional)

1/4 to 1/2 cup whole milk, half-and-half, or heavy (whipping) cream

5 tablespoons butter, preferably unsalted

3 to 5 tablespoons crème fraîche, sour cream, or heavy (whipping) cream

Salt and black pepper

2 to 3 tablespoons chopped chives, or thinly sliced green onions (optional)

1 Cook the potatoes and the whole garlic cloves in water to cover over medium-high heat until tender, for about 15 to 20 minutes.

2 Drain the potatoes and cooked garlic cloves, and either mash them or put through a ricer or sieve.

3 Heat the milk until bubbles form around the edge, then pour into the potatoes and mix together, over medium-low heat; then beat in the butter and crème fraîche, and season to taste with salt and pepper. If using, add the raw garlic, then mix in the chives.

4 Serve right away.

Variations

Garlic mashed potatoes are bliss. But they are just the beginning; add Jerusalem artichokes, add celeriac, stir in some spinach . . . oh, yummm. Garlic mashed potatoes are an entire category of deliciousness.

Jerusalem Artichoke Mash

Also known as sunchokes, Jerusalem artichokes (tubers related to sunflowers) have a nutty, earthy quality and are delicious in potato dishes such as gratins and mash. To prepare: Decrease the amount of potatoes by half and add an equivalent amount of Jerusalem artichokes. Parboil Jerusalem artichokes to loosen their skin; they are too difficult to peel when raw. Place 1 pound whole Jerusalem artichokes (or large pieces) in a saucepan with cold water to cover and a few drops of lemon juice. Bring to a boil and cook until they are half tender, for about 15 minutes. Drain and refresh under cold water, until they are cool enough to handle. When cool they should peel easily; discard the peels and use a paring knife for any bits of skin that are reluctant to slip away. Cut the peeled Jerusalem artichokes into pieces about the same size as the potatoes, and add them to the saucepan along with the potatoes. Bring to a boil and proceed as directed, mashing them with the garlic and butter and cream. Get your spoon and bowl ready for bliss. Very good with roasted duck.

Purée of Celery Root (Celeriac) Mashed Potatoes

This is a sort of creamy, earthy, spoon-it-into-your-mouth-and-swoon kind of dish. It makes a wonderful accompaniment for dark, richly meaty roasts or braises. Prepare the recipe as directed, omitting half the quantity of potatoes and substituting 1 medium celery root, about 1 1/2 pounds, peeled of its thick knobbly skin and cut into bite-size pieces. Cook it along with the potatoes. Instead of crème fraîche, use heavy (whipping) cream and omit the chopped raw garlic at the end. Serve sprinkled with chives.

Artichoke Mash

Decrease the amount of potatoes by about a third and add 2 artichokes, trimmed down to their hearts and cut into bite-size pieces. Cook the artichokes with the potatoes and garlic cloves, then drain and mash. I love this with roast chicken.

Spinach and Garlic Mashed Potatoes

Sounds ordinary, but it's beyond deliciousness. I've even made it with steakhouse leftovers, and it was great. Add 1 cup cooked, squeezed-dry, buttered spinach to your garlic mashed potatoes. Toss together and warm through. Sometimes I warm the spinach in chopped garlic and butter together before I stir it into the potatoes.

Garlic Mashed Potatoes with a Whiff of Casablanca

Nuggets of preserved lemon give a tangy, fragrant edge to rich garlic mash. Prepare garlic mashed potatoes as directed; then fold in the chopped rinsed peel of 2 Moroccan preserved lemons and 2 chopped garlic cloves, with a big dab or two of butter and a wedge of lemon for squirting, if desired.

That Ol' Mashed Potato Blues

Puréed blue potatoes, a creamy almost electric blue, very fetching. Keep the peel on to keep the color in. When they are just tender, drain as directed. Peel if you like, though I quite like the taste and texture of potato skins in my mash, and proceed as instructed. You can keep or omit the chives.

Oh La La, Those Pommes de Terres! That Fromage!

Add as much delectable Roquefort as you desire into your warm garlicky mash. Don't cook it together, simply let the cheese melt into the hot potatoes. Close your eyes and plop a spoonful right into your mouth. Mmmmmm. Have the rare roasted lamb ready.

Lebanese Garlic Mashed Potatoes (Batata Madooa Siyeme)

Omit the milk, butter, and crème fraîche, adding lemon juice to taste and increasing the extra-virgin olive oil to taste. Serve sprinkled with about 3 tablespoons finely chopped fresh mint instead of chives.

Crushed Potatoes
with Olive Oil

○ ● ○ ◐ ○ ●

For this recipe, inspired by my travels through France, you want to keep the potatoes only lightly crushed, in little chunks, rather than mashed. Take a bite; think Provence. This is delish with almost anything, from grilled lamb to steamed lobster, and even better eaten on its own as its own separate course. This is good at room temperature, too.

◇ Serves 4

6 medium-size waxy, white-skinned potatoes (1 to 1½ pounds), whole and unpeeled

½ to ¾ cup heavy (whipping) cream

Salt and pepper

2 to 3 tablespoons extra-virgin olive oil

1 to 2 tablespoons chopped chives

1 Place the potatoes in a heavy saucepan with cold water to cover. Bring to a boil, then reduce the heat to a steady low boil, or simmer, until the potatoes are just cooked through and still very firm, for about 15 to 20 minutes. Test them at 10 minutes; they are ready when a fork can just pierce them; you want them to keep their character and body when you warm them through with the cream.

2 Drain the potatoes. With a fork, break each potato up into about three pieces, and lightly crush parts of the potatoes, leaving big chunks.

3 Place the potatoes in a big nonstick skillet in one layer. Add the cream and warm through; cook over medium-high heat for about 5 minutes or long enough for the cream to thicken and be pretty much absorbed by the potatoes. Season to taste with salt and pepper.

4 Drizzle the olive oil on to the potatoes and mix lightly. Sprinkle with the chives and serve.

Variation
Potato Mash with Beans, Olive Oil, and Rosemary

Omit the cream and reduce the number of potatoes to 4; add 1 cup or so cooked pinto- or cranberry-type beans. Coarsely mash together, and add a few tablespoons of olive oil as directed, a few chopped garlic cloves, and a tablespoon or two of chopped fresh rosemary. You could use canned pinto beans, but wonderful home-cooked beans make all the difference. I recommend Rancho Gordo's New World Vegetables for all manner of beans, especially pinto-type. He grows them himself, and they are quite possibly the most delicious beans you'll ever munch. Steve Sando—also known as Rancho Gordo—and Paula Wolfert, cookbook author extraordinaire, have shared with me the secret to the best beans in the world, regardless of their type and method of growing. Here it is: Cook the beans in a clay pot. The difference it makes is astounding!

Irresistible Basil Mashed Potatoes to Make You Swoon

○ ● ○ ● ○ ●

For years I made basil mashed potatoes using pesto or puréed raw basil, then a few years ago
at Le Cordon Bleu in Paris, I noticed that the chef blanched his basil leaves first, before puréeing.
While I had until then thought that raw basil definitely gives the best flavor and aroma, one bite
of the chef's potatoes proved me wrong: Blanching imparts the most refined, sleek, and strong flavor
of basil you could desire. And yes, the recipe uses a lot of cream; it's sooooo worth it.

Serve with duck or lamb, or use as a bed for Italian sausages. But truthfully,
the potatoes are also divine just eaten from a bowl.

◇ Serves 4 to 6

2 pounds floury, baking-type potatoes, peeled and cut into chunks

Salt

2 to 3 cups fresh basil leaves of any type (2 to 3 ounces—a nice big bunch)

2 cups heavy (whipping) cream or half-and-half

4 tablespoons butter

Black pepper

1 Place the potatoes in a saucepan and fill with water to cover. Add a big pinch of salt. Bring to a boil and cook, covered, for about 10 minutes, or until the potatoes are just tender. Drain, return to the heat, and shake for a few minutes to dry them out; turn off the heat, cover the pan, and keep warm.

2 Meanwhile, blanch the basil. Plunge it into a saucepan of boiling water, cook a moment or two until the leaves wilt and slightly change color, and lift out of the pot using a slotted spoon, then plunge into a bowl of ice water. Leave for about five minutes or until it turns brightly colored, then lift from the ice water.

3 Heat the cream in a saucepan until bubbles form around the edge of the pan.

4 Squeeze the basil in your hands gently to rid it of excess water from cooking. Place in a food processor and whirl to purée. Slowly pour the hot cream into this puréed basil and whirl until it forms a fragrant, pale green cream.

5 Coarsely mash the potatoes with a masher, then add the basil cream and mash it in; work in the butter, and season to taste with salt and pepper. If you're serving duck or lamb, serve the potatoes with a drizzle of the port reduction around the edge.

The Prince's Potatoes:
Mexican Mash from Highgrove

○ ● ○ ◉ ○ ●

Here is how I ended up with the prince's potatoes: I was invited to visit Highgrove, HRH Prince Charles's organic estate in Gloucestershire, and as I was tromping through the fields with His Royal Highness's gardener, David Wilson, listening to the cows chew, marveling at the wild flora and fauna that are left on the edges of the plantings to encourage a good balance of natural pest control, David mentioned that HRH Prince Charles had some very nice potatoes growing. "Omigod!" I cried, "I need potatoes for tomorrow, I'm cooking on the air (BBC Radio 4). Our theme is potatoes!" I was given a shovel and set free in His Royal Highness's garden, digging up and taking away a small bag full of Prince Charles's spuds. The next day there I was, on the radio, cooking the potatoes according to the following recipe. It was a freewheeling show, devoted to being exuberant with vegetables, and I thought that Mexican-inspired mash might be just the thing for the potatoes—and anyhow, I was in a Mexican mood. I would imagine that Prince Charles would be surprised to see his potatoes cooked like this, though I'd like to think he'd be pleased. You may use whichever type of potatoes are your favorites for mashing; Highgrove's were somewhere in between a mealy baking type and a waxy one, and ever so tasty.

◇ Serves 4 to 6

2 poblano chiles, or 1 Anaheim plus 1 green bell pepper

3 pounds potatoes, any type

Sugar and salt

10 cooked tomatillos, or several tablespoons very mild green salsa (optional)

5 garlic cloves, chopped

5 to 6 tablespoons extra-virgin olive oil

¼ teaspoon cumin seeds, or more

2 to 4 tablespoons sour cream (low-fat is fine)

Lime juice

3 to 4 tablespoons chopped cilantro

Black pepper

continued

continued

1 Roast the chiles over an open flame until the skin chars; place in a plastic or paper bag or a bowl, and cover or seal well. Leave to sweat for at least 30 minutes, then peel the skin off. Remove the stem and seeds and coarsely chop. Set aside.

2 Rinse the potatoes to wash off the dirt, then cut into chunks; peel if you like, but I prefer the flavor of skin in my potato. If you like the flavor of skin but not the texture, cook the potatoes whole or in halves, then remove the skin when cooked.

3 Add water to cover, then a pinch of sugar and salt. Bring to a boil, reduce the heat to medium-high, and cook until the potatoes are just tender.

4 Drain, then place the potatoes back on the stove, over medium heat, shaking every so often for a few minutes to dry them out.

5 Mash the potatoes coarsely with a masher or strong fork. When they are chunkily mashed, add the cooked tomatillos, (if using), the garlic, olive oil, reserved roasted chiles, cumin seeds, sour cream, lime juice to taste, and cilantro. Season to taste with salt and pepper.

Variation
Maharaja Mash

For curry flavors added to your mash, prepare as directed, using tomato salsa instead of tomatillos. Then lightly sauté the garlic in the olive oil instead of adding it raw, and sprinkle on about 1 teaspoon cumin, 1 teaspoon curry powder, $1/2$ teaspoon ground ginger, and $1/2$ teaspoon turmeric as the garlic warms in the oil. Add this mixture to the potatoes, and instead of sour cream add yogurt, then stir in the lime juice and cilantro as in the main recipe. This is delicious stuffed into a roasted red bell pepper for a rather fetching presentation; eat it cold, or drizzle it with olive oil and warm in the oven just before serving.

Aligot

Mashed Potatoes Whipped into a Garlic Frenzy with Lots of Melty Cheese

○ ● ○ ◐ ○ ◐

This Auvergnat dish—from France's rugged, rural southwest—is authentically made with the local Cantal cheese, but a combination of mozzarella, Cheddar, Jack, and ricotta is delicious, too. I've used a combination of Wensleydale, white Cheddar or Havarti, and cottage cheese, in the U.K. Serve the Aligot hot and steaming in bowls, its melted cheese stringing as you spoon it up.

◇ Serves 4 to 6

6 baking potatoes (about 2½ pounds), peeled and cut into chunks

4 tablespoons butter

¾ cup hot milk

6 to 7 garlic cloves, chopped

12 ounces Cantal or a combination of mixed cheeses, such as Cheddar, mozzarella, or Jack

½ to ¾ cup ricotta cheese

Salt and pepper

1 Cook the potatoes in rapidly boiling salted water until they are tender, for about 20 minutes. Drain and mash with a fork or potato masher.

2 Over low heat, mash in the butter, milk, and half the garlic, then add the cheese, beating with a wooden spoon as it melts, until it becomes a delectable stringy mess. Season to taste with salt and pepper.

3 Add the remaining garlic and serve it all in warmed bowls, with spoons.

Baked, Roasted & Gratinéed:

As a Sideshow or Main Event

7

Baked Potatoes

Use floury potatoes, preferably large ones. Make a hole or two in each potato so that it doesn't explode. For a crisp skin, I don't oil or butter the outside; for a softer skin, do rub the outside with oil or butter. Place the potatoes in a hot oven, say 425°F, for about an hour; if they are very large, an hour and a half; if they are smaller, less time. If you need to pace the potatoes, lower the heat and cook them longer and slower. The potatoes are ready when you can pierce them with a fork or sharp skewer. For a thick, crunchy skin and very tender flesh, let the potatoes cool in the oven after you have turned off the heat. Ditto for the embers of a fire: tuck whole potatoes into the dying embers—on their own or wrapped in foil—and let them slowly, slowly roast on the coals. You can leave them in for 30 minutes to start, testing every so often by fishing one out and cutting into it. When they come out, they will have a thick skin and tender flesh.

Baked potatoes can be helped along by precooking in a microwave, though true aficionados are not keen on that. It depends on how desperate you are for a baked potato, as it does change the flesh somewhat, to a slightly more moist and sticky interior. Also, you need to do the microwaving one potato at a time. Wash, dry, and prick the potato— 8 ounces or so—and nuke it for 3 to 4 minutes at full power. Let it sit for a few minutes, then place in a hot oven to finish for about 20 minutes. You can, alternatively, cook it all the way through in the microwave; allow 6 minutes.

To open potatoes for maximum fluffiness, cut into them with only a few stabs of the paring knife and making a cross shape—the cross shape rather than a single slash helps the potato flesh fluff out of its skin. Using a clean cloth, hold the potato and pinch the bottom hard, so that the insides smoosh up and out a bit of the potato, giving a maximum fluff spilling out of the spud. Now that is something to explore with your butter pats.

Yummy Things to Put on Baked Potatoes

The classic: Butter, sour cream, and chives or green onions. A great addition: a little shredded smoked salmon or briny caviar for a saline edge.

Uncle Sy's chile potatoes: Spicy chile con carne, shredded cheese, and chopped onions, spooned over an opened, fluffed potato.

Aioli: Topped with plain aioli, or saffron or herb variations.

Truffle butter (or chile butter, or garlic butter, or mixed herb butter).

Olive butter: A tablespoon or two of black or green olive paste mashed with about 3 tablespoons unsalted butter at room temperature; with garlic or herbs, or both, as desired; spooned into the fluffy flesh of a hot baked potato.

A poached egg with some spunky salsa.

Raw foie gras sliced into slivers when partially frozen. Or foie gras *mi-cuit* (partially cooked), also best when partially frozen and sliced paper thin, or cooked foie gras, to melt in delicately in the heat of the hot, dry, fluffy-fleshed baked potato; a few shakes of good truffle oil to pair ever-so-nicely with the melting foie gras on your potato.

A sprinkle of wine vinegar and a handful of young pea greens. Or purslane, or other sweet green lettuce.

Greek yogurt: Seasoned with paprika and cumin.

Extra-virgin olive oil and pinch of *za'atar:* Middle Eastern spice mixture of wild thyme, sumac, cumin, coriander, and toasted sesame seeds. A little crumbed feta cheese is tasty with this earthy potato, too.

How to Make the Best Oven Fries

Peel or don't peel—the choice is yours—about 2 pounds of floury baking potatoes, such as russets, into french-fry shapes, about 1/2 inch wide and 1/4 inch thick. Place in a large bowl and cover with water to soak; you don't *need* to soak, but I think that the result is crisper, lighter, and crustier when you do. For cold tap water, you'll want to soak for 1 hour; for a quickie soak, use hot tap water, and you'll need only 10 minutes for truly wonderful results.

Preheat the oven to 475°F.

Drizzle several tablespoons oil of choice on a shallow-sided baking sheet (12 x 18 inches) or two, depending on how well the potatoes fit in a single uncrowded layer. A lightweight pan doesn't brown potatoes thoroughly; use a heavyweight pan for a browned, even, crunchy result.

Sprinkle the bottom of the baking sheet with about 1/2 to 1 teaspoon coarse or flaked sea salt.

Drain the potatoes and dry with a clean towel or paper towels. Toss them with 1 to 2 tablespoons vegetable, canola, peanut, or olive oil, then spread in a single layer. Cover with foil and place in the oven; bake for 5 to 10 minutes.

Remove the foil and return to the oven for another 10 minutes or until the tops are turning golden brown, then using a spatula, turn the potatoes and return them to the oven to bake for a further 10 to 15 minutes, or until golden brown. Serve at once.

A Bed of Potatoes

Other Things to Sprinkle Oven Fries With

- Malt vinegar for fish and chips or for a British experience, or tarragon vinegar, or truffle vinegar because it is so delectable
- Moroccan *chermoula* (page 51)
- Chopped garlic, green onion, and cilantro
- Chile or enchilada sauce plus shredded cheese, chopped onions, cilantro, and pickled chiles—in Dixon, California, they call this Papas Locas (Crazy Potatoes)!
- Finely chopped ginger and garlic added during the last 10 minutes; salt and hot chile flakes to taste

Roasting a fish? A leg of lamb? A succulent chicken? Duck legs? Cod fillets Greek style? Roast them on top of a bed of potatoes, and the savory juices will permeate the potatoes as well as the meat, fish, or poultry. Make a bed of thinly sliced potatoes on the bottom of the pan, scattered with aromatics such as thinly sliced garlic, sprigs of fresh thyme or rosemary, thinly sliced onions or tomatoes, or both, and thin slices of lemon, then top with your delicious thing. For a large piece of meat like leg of lamb, preroast the lamb about halfway before you place it on its bed of potatoes; for a fish, chicken, or duck legs, they will probably cook at the same time; for fillets of cod or other small portions, preroast the potatoes, drizzling them with olive oil and sprinkling them with salt first. When the potatoes are almost tender, top with the fish and return to the oven for a further 10 minutes or so, to finish roasting.

The British Husband's Best Roast Potatoes

What is a Sunday lunch without roast potatoes? Essence of sadness for a Brit, I can assure you. Roast potatoes are one of the best parts of the meal, the thing that accompanies the golden chicken or the roast beef, and sometimes the thing that is very delicious when the other things don't turn out. My husband is brilliant with his roasted potatoes. Over the years he has perfected his talent for this dish and changed over from an ordinary sunflower or vegetable oil to olive oil. Oh, what a delicious difference it makes! Of course, if you have duck, goose, or bacon fat, slosh some of that delicious stuff into the pan instead of, or in addition to, the olive oil.

For the potatoes, you can choose any type you like. Floury baking types of potatoes will give a light and fluffy interior, while waxy potatoes will be creamier when you bite into them. The outsides should be crunchy no matter what. The only type of potato that I personally don't like for roasting is the slightly sweet red-skinned potato that is so good for salad.

To serve four, preheat the oven to 350°F to 400°F, boil about 2 1/2 pounds unpeeled potatoes, cut into chunks or quarters, place in water to cover with a pinch of both salt and sugar, and cook until the potatoes are halfway cooked, that is, still crunchy on the inside. The timing depends on the size and age of the potatoes. Drain the boiled potatoes thoroughly, then arrange in a baking pan with a raised edge so that they are not touching each other, and drizzle generously with olive oil, about 1/3 cup. Sprinkle generously with sea salt, preferably flakes or large grains, and scatter a head of garlic, broken up into cloves and peeled, throughout the pan, in between the potato chunks. Roast for about an hour, depending on the size of the potatoes. They are done when they are crunchy golden brown on the outside and the garlic cloves are crunchy and creamy and browned. Serve right away.

(A Spanish mother's variation: cut peeled potatoes in half lengthwise, then score the cut sides deeply with a knife. Rub with olive oil and sprinkle with salt, then roast as directed).

Gratin Girl's Potatoes:
Classic Potato Gratin

○ ● ○ ● ○ ●

One day I answered the buzzing doorbell. Standing there was my friend Emma, the "gratin girl" of the title—bag of potatoes in her arms, butter and cream in her tote bag. "The weather is beastly," said Emma. "I gotta make a gratin." There was no stopping her; she soaked potatoes, slathered butter, rubbed garlic, all accompanied to the sound of wine swishing in glasses and gurgling down throats. She made a huge gratin, in a big rustic ceramic baking casserole, and, our shame having left us earlier in the evening, we sat down to eat the delicious monster at the unset table, armed with spoons. I did make a salad just for good form, but dinner that night was all about the gratin. And it was divine.

This potato gratin is absolutely classic, and simplicity itself: no onions, no cheese topping, just potatoes, bathed in butter and cream, with a bit of garlic for oomph. It's the sort of thing you just might find as an enticing slab next to roasted or stewed meat, chicken, or duck, in a wintertime Parisian bistro.

◇ Serves 4 to 6

3½ to 4 pounds baking potatoes, peeled and thinly sliced

4 tablespoons butter, cut into small pieces, plus extra for the casserole

3 to 5 garlic cloves, chopped

Salt and pepper

1 cup heavy (whipping) cream

2 tablespoons chopped fresh parsley, or chives, for garnish

1 Place the sliced potatoes in a bowl with cold water to cover. Leave for at least 30 minutes, or up to an hour. Remove from the cloudy water, and dry with a clean towel.

2 Preheat the oven to 375°F.

3 Butter the bottom and sides of an earthenware baking casserole, about 3½ inches deep, and large enough to fit all the potatoes (very large). If you have no round ceramic pan, use an ordinary baking pan. Sprinkle about half the garlic along the edges of the buttered sides of the pan.

continued

continued

4 Make a layer of potatoes, dot with butter pieces, sprinkle with salt and pepper, drizzle with a few spoonfuls of cream, scatter a little garlic on top, then repeat in this fashion until all the potatoes have been used. End the top with a dabbing of butter, the last slosh of cream, and a sprinkling of salt and pepper.

5 Bake for an hour to an hour and a half, or until the potatoes are very tender and have absorbed all the cream; the top of the potatoes should be golden brown with darker brown splotches here and there. This is a very rustic dish and by its very nature is very forgiving timewise; if you need more time, lower the oven's heat, and to speed the cooking up and give it a nice dark topping, raise the heat to 400°F for the last 10 to 15 minutes.

6 Serve in its own casserole, or dish up individual portions, sprinkling each with a little chopped fresh parsley.

Variations

Potato Gratin with A Scattering of Fragrant Herbs

Once in a bistro I ate a similar gratin sprinkled with 2 table-spoons chopped fresh tarragon and chervil in addition to the chives, as well as a teaspoon or two of pink peppercorns. It was lovely!

Dublin Coddle

This is a sort of gratin layered with sausages and bacon, and cooked with broth instead of cream. Layer the potatoes with about 12 ounces of Irish sausages (or British bangers) cut into bite-size pieces, and about 12 ounces of good lean Irish bacon, diced, or French lardons, along with a couple of onions, thinly sliced. Cover with a cup or two of beef, chicken, or vegetable broth (or water plus a bouillon cube or two), and sprinkle with a little thyme. Cover and bake for an hour. Remove the cover, dot the top with butter, and return to the oven for another 30 minutes or until the tops of the potatoes are crusty and browned and the potatoes underneath creamy and tender. Serve hot, sprinkled with chopped fresh parsley.

Roquefort Potato Gratin

Do as they (sometimes) do in France's southwest—add a big jolt of Roquefort or another salty, briny, pungent, and delicious cheese to your gratin. Layer about 6 ounces in between the slices of potato, butter, garlic, and cream.

Jannson's Temptation

The Swedish classic gratin is a basic creamy gratin, inter-spersed with lots of soft sautéed onions and lots and lots of chopped anchovies, then baked. It's warming on a freezing night after you've drunk abundantly of aquavit.

It's All About the Potatoes!
Potatoey Gratin

○ ● ○ ◐ ○ ●

This gratin is more like a potato cake in that it is not awash with cream; rather, the thinly sliced potatoes are held together by their own potato-ness. It has a whiff of garlic, a crisp golden top, and a creamy potatoey interior, with tiny flecks of salt for a saline crunch. Sometimes I dust the top with a bit of cumin, sometimes not—both ways are divine and I can't decide which version I like better! You'll have to do what I do and make two, one with and one without. Or simply sprinkle only half with cumin and let each person choose. I like a good-flavored yellow-fleshed succulent potato such as Yukon Gold or Inca Gold.

This dish was first inspired by a potato and white-cheese gratin I ate in Bulgaria (and ate and ate), though its overriding character is Pommes Anna, in that it's all about the potatoes. As potato gratins go, this is surprisingly light to eat, and extremely easy to make. And very tasty indeed.

◇ Serves 4

1½ to 2 pounds yellow-fleshed potatoes (see headnote)
4 tablespoons extra-virgin olive oil, or as needed
3 to 4 garlic cloves, chopped
Coarse sea salt and coarsely ground black pepper
4 to 6 tablespoons crème fraîche
Ground cumin for sprinkling (optional)

1 Preheat the oven to 400°F.

2 Peel and thinly slice the potatoes, preferably lengthwise as it is easier to layer and looks prettier, too. Unless your potatoes are very starchy, don't bother soaking or rinsing them—you want a little bit of starch to hold the potatoes together.

3 Lightly drizzle about a tablespoon of the olive oil in the bottom of a 9- to 11-inch pie or cake pan, then sprinkle the bottom with a little of the garlic, and over that, make a layer of slightly overlapping potatoes. Sprinkle lightly with sea salt and pepper, then make another layer of potatoes. Repeat four times or so, sprinkling a little garlic every so often, then make a few dabs of crème fraîche as you layer. It doesn't matter how you do it, really; you just want an uneven streak of crème fraîche and a whiff of garlic here and there. End with a layer of the potatoes, a drizzle of olive oil, and a sprinkle of salt and pepper.

4 Bake in the oven for about 30 minutes or until the top is lightly golden and the potatoes are just tender.

5 If using cumin, sprinkle with a pinch of it and return to the oven for a minute or so to warm up the spice's fragrance.

6 Serve hot.

Variations

Classic Pommes Anna

Use a floury, white-fleshed potato. Omit the olive oil, garlic, crème fraîche, and cumin, and use butter instead. Layer the unsoaked potatoes—you want that potato starch to help stick the thin slices together—with butter. Use 1½ to 2 pounds floury baking potatoes, peeled, as directed, and dot each layer with 7 to 8 tablespoons unsalted butter and a little salt and pepper.

Thin Potato Galette

Another classy classic, this is the same dish as Pommes Anna, but made in a larger, flatter size, and only about 2 or 3 rounds high; you end up with a delicate, crispy-edged potato-slice disc, or galette.

Provençal Tomato-Scented Potato Gratin

Layer this olive oil–scented gratin with about 6 garlic cloves and 1 to 1½ pounds thinly sliced (or canned diced) tomatoes. Omit the cumin, and use a pinch of fresh herbs or dried oregano instead.

Note: Any of the gratins can be made in individual-sized ramekins, baking at a slightly elevated oven temperature, 425°F instead of 400°F.

Patatas me Limono

Greek Lemon-Garlic Potatoes

○ ● ○ ◗ ○ ●

Everyone has his or her own way of making this dish—some place the potatoes around a roasting chunk of lamb or goat, others around a chicken or chunks of fish. Recently, I watched television chef and Greek culinary guru Vefa Alexandriou make potatoes with fish on her daily cooking show. I watched her put them in the oven for a segment the next day and when everyone was going home—the program was finished taping—I wanted to stay until the next day when she would finish cooking the potatoes! They looked so appealing next to that fish. The important thing all agree on is that the potatoes get bathed every so often with lemon juice, plus a big squeeze at the end. That and lots of olive oil.

Bake it for a longer time with a larger amount of water for a softer, more falling-apart quality to the potatoes, though this—and the length of time they take to cook through—will depend on what type of potatoes you are using. This is at its best using Greek potatoes, the yellowish moist and succulent variety that reminds me of Peruvian potatoes, but any medium potato that is not too waxy, not too floury, will do.

◇ Serves 4

2 to 2 1/2 pounds all-purpose potatoes (see headnote), peeled and cut into thick fingers or wedges

1/4 to 1/2 cup extra-virgin olive oil, as needed

3 lemons

Sea salt

1/2 to 1 teaspoon Greek oregano, crumbled between your hands

Black pepper

5 to 8 garlic cloves, thickly sliced

1 Preheat the oven to 400°F. In a large baking pan, arrange the potato pieces and cover with about 1/2 inch water. Drizzle with half the olive oil and the juice of 1 lemon, tossing the lemon rinds into the pan alongside the potatoes. Sprinkle to taste with sea salt, oregano, and pepper, and place in the oven for about 20 minutes.

2 Squeeze the second lemon over the potatoes, adding the rind, toss the potatoes around using a spatula, taking care not to break them up too much, and scatter the pieces of garlic around the pan. Add more olive oil if needed. Return to the oven.

3 Bake for another 15 minutes or so, remove from the oven, toss around a bit, then return for another five minutes.

4 Remove from the oven, squeeze the last lemon over the top, and scrape all the yummy pan juices up along with the potatoes. Serve right away (though they're not bad at room temperature either).

Variation
Gravy-Soaked Roasted Potatoes

Instead of lemon juice, add about $1/2$ cup or so beef or turkey gravy to the pan when the potatoes are about half cooked through. Continue to bake together, as the potatoes absorb the gravy and thicken it, while the gravy gives the potatoes a deliciously meaty meatiness.

Edouard's Frankfurt
Book Fair Gratin
also known as Pommes à la Vignerons

○ ● ○ ● ○ ●

A lusty casserole of the grape pickers and wine makers, and—it would seem—publishers,
it's hard to know which name to call it, because to me it is both of the above names, depending on
who is making it and where I am eating it. It only differs according to surroundings and cheeses.
In the wine country, this lusty casserole, which the grape pickers stoke up on during the hard work of the
vendange, or the harvest, will be made with a local Gruyère or other mountain cheese. If it's the
publishers' version you want, then you must go to Germany where each year Edouard Cointreau,
of the World Gourmand Awards and the *International Cookbook Revue*, serves this gratin at his
annual bash, usually made with local German cheeses such as Bergkaese.

This is a sort of potatoey gratin that is made in a zillion other kitchens, and once you've got the idea,
it's hard not to want to get your cholesterol checked, then head into the kitchen with mountains of potatoes,
vats of cream, and hunks of cheese. (I'll share a secret: each year I know an editor who goes to the
Frankfurt Book Fair thinking a little about the business she hopes will come her way, but thinking *a lot* about
the gratin that Edouard serves at his annual bash. Get on the invitation list if you can! Potatoes await!)

The potatoes are layered with nubbins of bacon or ham, splashed with a whiff of wine, cosseted
with cream, and slathered with melted cheese all over the place. The top gets crusty, the inside gets
smooooshy, and it's simply delish. I like a combination of Cheddar and Emmentaler or Appenzeller.

◇ Serves 4

2 tablespoons butter, plus extra for the pan

2 garlic cloves, chopped

4 medium-size baking potatoes (about 2 pounds)

2 medium onions, or 4 shallots, thinly sliced or chopped

3 to 4 ounces unsmoked ham, or bacon, cut into lardons or bite-size morsels

Small grating of nutmeg

8 to 10 ounces cheese, such as a combination of Cheddar and Emmentaler or Appenzeller, shredded

¼ cup dry white wine, with a good acidity, or milk

1 to 1½ cups heavy (whipping) cream or half-and-half

1 tablespoon finely chopped fresh rosemary

Salt and black pepper

1 Butter the inside of a large ceramic or metal baking pan, then rub with the garlic.

2 Preheat the oven to 375°F to 400°F.

3 Peel and thinly slice the potatoes. Make 3 layers of the potatoes, onions, ham, nutmeg, the garlic used to rub the pan, and the cheese, ending with the cheese. Pour on the wine and cream, and sprinkle with rosemary. Season to taste with salt and pepper, keeping in mind that the ham and cheese are salty. Dot the top with the 2 tablespoons of butter.

4 Bake for 30 to 40 minutes, or until the top is golden browned and the potatoes are tender; if they are not tender, and it is very likely they will not be, lower the heat to 325°F and continue to bake for about 30 minutes more. When the potatoes are just tender (test them by piercing the top with a bamboo skewer) remove from the oven and let sit for a few minutes before you serve it.

5 Serve hot.

Variations

Potato-Broccoli Gratin

Add a layer of thinly sliced broccoli somewhere in the middle of the potatoes.

Mexican Potato Gratin with Chipotle Cream

Omit the ham, nutmeg, wine, and rosemary. Layer the potatoes and onions with the cheeses—you might wish to use Jack, Romano, or a combination, instead of the Emmentaler or Appenzeller. You could also add a little goat cheese if you like —it's optional—say, 6 ounces sliced or crumbled. Sprinkle with chipotle salsa from a bottle as you go along, end with a layer of shredded cheese, and bake as directed.

Auntie Stellie's Twice-Baked
Thanksgiving Potatoes

○ ● ○ ◑ ● ○ ◐

For just giving thanks (thanks for potatoes!), this is almost a culinary version of "You can never go home again," or rather, in this case—you can.

Let me explain: Some things never taste as good when you grow up as they did when you were a child. That's why this dish of baked potatoes—the flesh hollowed out and mashed with butter, crème fraîche, and green onions, then topped with melty cheese—is such a treat. It's the dish my Auntie Stellie, of cheese and dill pickle sandwich fame, always made for Thanksgiving at her house, the celebrations in which the number of guests were never counted, merely welcomed. She also made fabulous Jell-O molds.

Next to the stuffing, to which I was also devoted, the hot stuffed potatoes were the best part of the meal. They might be quintessentially American Thanksgiving in style, but they certainly have international appeal. Recently, I was describing these potatoes to a friend, cookbook author Maria Villegas from Colombia, where potatoes are indigenous and eaten at nearly every meal. When I came to the part about the cream and the onions and the cheese, she cried out: "We make these in Bogotá!" And while visiting Athens, Greece, what's that I see? Twice-baked potatoes, with spinach and feta cheese (see variation on page 126).

This version serves 4 to 6, but you can multiply it at will. Twice-baked potatoes for 50 are just as good as for 2. Feel free to adjust amounts, since no one potato is the same size as the next; even if it weighs the same, it may need more or less butter and crème fraîche. Three things: (1) do not be tempted to use low-fat substitutes or—*alors!*—margarine; (2) do not be tempted to use a food processor to mash and mix the potatoes—you'll get instant glue and that glue will absorb the sour cream and onion; and (3) err on the side of generosity with the butter, crème fraîche, green onions, and, heck, the cheese, too. Any excess cheese melts off and into the pan and forms crispy little cheese cracker-like things of deliciousness. Nibble them yourself or peel them out of the pan and set them next to the potatoes as a yummy lagniappe.

continued

continued

◇ Serves 4 to 6

4 to 6 medium-size creamy-fleshed baking potatoes (5 to 6 inches long, 6 ounces each)

6 tablespoons unsalted butter

6 to 8 tablespoons crème fraîche

6 to 7 green onions, thinly sliced

Sea salt and freshly ground black pepper

6 to 8 ounces Double Gloucester or mature Cheddar, shredded

Paprika, for sprinkling on top

1 Bake the potatoes (see page 111).

2 When cool enough to handle, use a teaspoon to scoop out their insides, leaving a perimeter of potato flesh next to the skin all the way around.

3 Preheat the oven to 400°F.

4 Coarsely mash all the potato flesh in a bowl, then add the butter, crème fraîche, and green onions and mix together. Season to taste with salt and pepper.

5 Spoon the mixture evenly into the potatoes, then arrange in a single layer in a baking pan and sprinkle with the cheese. Top with a pinch of paprika on each, then bake for about 10 minutes, or long enough to melt and sizzle the cheese on top of the potatoes and warm the potatoes all the way through.

Variations

Patates me Spanaki e Tyri

Prepare as directed, only reduce the crème fraîche to 3 tablespoons (or use cottage cheese), and add about 1 cup cooked spinach, squeeze dried and chopped, several tablespoons chopped fresh dill, and about $1/2$ cup or more feta cheese. Keep the green onions; they are just so good in twice-baked potatoes. Fill the hollowed-out potato skins, then top with the cheese as directed, using a Greek *kasseri*, *kashkeval*, or *kefalotyri*, or Monterey Jack or Sonoma Jack, instead of Cheddar. Bake the stuffed potatoes as directed.

Maria Villegas's Twice-Baked Potatoes

Colombian chef and food writer Maria Villegas—who truly is too beautiful and calm to be a mere mortal, let alone a chef who trained at the chicest restaurants of Europe and the United States—prepares these potatoes using cream cheese instead of sour cream, and doesn't usually top it with a melted cheese but rather makes the potato filling smooth, so it bakes to a smooth crust on top. Sometimes Maria tops each little twice-baked potato with a big twirl of supple, saline-smoked salmon and a scattering of chives or capers.

Silvena Rowe's Wild Mushroom Variation from Bulgaria

Add sautéed sliced wild mushrooms, or a mixture of domestic ordinary mushrooms and refrigerated dried porcini, to the mashed potato mix, and Jack or *kashkeval* instead of Cheddar.

Gratin Forestier
Mighty Wild Mushroom Potato Gratin

○ ● ○ ◗ ○ ●

Your basic potato gratin, awash with cream, and oomphed up with a forest full of mushrooms.
It smells divine while it's cooking—and you won't be able to stop yourself from eating,
but try to; the leftovers are insanely good.

◇ Serves 6

4 large russet potatoes (about 1½ pounds), peeled and thinly sliced

3 tablespoons unsalted butter, plus extra for the gratin dish

8 ounces ordinary white or brown mushrooms, thinly sliced or chopped

1 large portobello, thinly sliced or chopped

2 fresh chanterelle mushrooms, or other exotic mushrooms, such as oyster or *trompette de la mort*

4 garlic cloves, chopped

Salt and pepper

2 shallots, peeled and chopped

½ to ¾ ounce dried porcini, broken up into small pieces

1½ cups chicken or vegetable stock or broth

1 cup heavy (whipping) cream

2 tablespoons chopped fresh chervil or parsley

1 Soak potatoes in water to cover for at least 10 minutes.

2 While you're doing that, heat the 3 tablespoons of butter in a large nonstick skillet over medium-high heat and sauté the ordinary mushrooms, the portobello, and the chanterelles, along with about half the garlic. Season to taste with salt and pepper and set aside.

3 Drain and pat the potatoes dry. Preheat the oven to 450°F.

4 Butter the bottom and sides of a gratin dish and sprinkle the remaining garlic on the bottom and sides, then layer the potatoes, shallots, crumbled dry porcini, and sautéed mushrooms about four times.

5 Pour the stock over the top, then the cream. Cover with foil and bake at 450°F for about 30 minutes. Remove the foil, raise the heat to 500°F, and bake off the liquid, for about 15 to 20 more minutes, until the top is golden brown, the potatoes are tender, and the liquid inside is a thick, almost custard-like, cloak for the potatoes.

6 Serve sprinkled with the chervil.

Kate's Hasselbacks
with Bajan Spicing

○ ● ○ ◖ ○ ●

My buddy Kate Goodwin, along with her partner in potatoes, Jane Milton, travels throughout the U.K. armed with pots and pans, charming little aprons, and boxes of spuds, cooking and demonstrating all the yummy things one can do with potatoes.

This recipe is a result of Kate's vacation from potatoes, to the Caribbean island of Barbados. Kate did a bit of snorkeling, then settled down in the island kitchens with the cooks. She came back with a glowing tan, and this potato dish—which shows that you can never really take a vacation from potatoes.

You cut the spuds in the fanned hasselback style, great for maximizing crunchiness, then coat them with a *bajan* seasoning paste (somewhat like jerk), and roast to deliciousness. I like to serve more of the fresh green paste alongside for dipping—when you run out of potatoes, it's good for just dipping in with your fingers! In fact, the hasselback is a Swedish dish, invented in Stockholm's Hasselbacken restaurant. The multiple cuts across the top of the potatoes provide a fan of crisp, crisp potato crunchiness, its bottom creamy like baked potato flesh. You can use either floury or waxy potatoes, and you can either peel the potatoes or leave them unpeeled. I opt for the latter, as not only is it easier, but I find that the peel is usually the crispest part of all.

◇ Serves 4 to 6

8 to 10 medium floury or waxy potatoes (1½ pounds), or about 30 new or other small oval potatoes, peeled or not

Bajan Seasoning Paste

8 garlic cloves

One 2-inch piece ginger, cut up or coarsely chopped

2 small onions, or 1 medium onion, chopped

4 green onions

1 teaspoon red pepper flakes, or several small, hot fresh chiles

½ green bell pepper

2 tablespoons chopped fresh parsley

1 tablespoon fresh thyme, or 2 teaspoons dried

4 to 5 tablespoons fresh mint, or 2 teaspoons dried

Sea salt and freshly ground black pepper

4 tablespoons extra-virgin olive oil, as needed

1 To cut the potatoes the hasselback way, place each potato into the bowl of a big soup spoon; put it in a direction that it will just about fit. With a knife, make deep cuts in the top, rounded part of the potato, cutting about $1/4$ inch deep; holding the potato in the spoon keeps the knife from going all the way through. You want the tops to be cut, but you want the potatoes held together at the bottoms. Alternatively, instead of a spoon you could cut the potatoes using a skewer; spear each potato with the skewer about $1/2$ inch from the bottom of the potato. Carefully slice down, stopping when you reach the skewer. As each potato is finished, place it in a bowl of cold (add a few ice cubes) water and keep cutting the potatoes. The cold water will help the potato slices to fan out and also rinse off the excess starch that could stick the slices back together when they bake. You can leave them like this for up to 2 hours.

2 Preheat the oven to 400°F.

3 Remove the potatoes from their watery bath and drain.

4 To make the *bajan* seasoning paste: In a food processor, combine the garlic, ginger, onions, green onions, red pepper flakes, bell pepper, parsley, thyme, and mint, a large pinch of salt, and lots of pepper. Whirl until it forms a smoothish paste.

5 Put a splodge of the *bajan* paste on the bottom of each potato, place it in a baking pan large enough to fit them all in a single layer spread out a bit, and spoon a tablespoon or two of the paste on top of each potato, too. Drizzle with olive oil, and sprinkle with a little extra salt.

6 Roast for about 35 to 45 minutes, or until the potatoes are golden brown and the edges have separated into crispy ridges. Baste with the hot oil once or twice; this helps the ridges to spread. If the potatoes and the spice mixture are threatening to burn, reduce the heat to about 350°F.

7 Serve each hasselback with a spoonful of the fresh *bajan* seasoning paste.

Variation
Stockholm Hasselbacks

If you are in the mood for hasselbacks but don't feel like jerk flavors, the traditional Swedish version is made with butter, goose or duck fat, and, instead of the spices, a wild scattering of freshly grated Parmesan and bread crumbs; they turn golden as the potatoes cook, making the whole thing even crunchier. Strew a handful of bay leaves over the bottom of the pan for an herbal perfume to the potatoes.

Fried

Alongside Anything!

8

in a Pan:

One heavy skillet, a sack of potatoes, and enough fat for browning: a recipe made for potato heaven. Truly, regardless of how much we love mashed potatoes (and we do, we do), or swoon over potato soup, or dig in to creamy gratins, or munch on crunchy roasted spuds, there is nothing more irresistible or quintessentially potato than potatoes that are fried.

French fries are probably the most famous potatoes in the world, and though the Belgians mumble about *frites* being their own, as do the British, I tend to believe the French when they say that these crisp batons of fried potatoes originated on the streets of Paris, near the Pont Neuf. The vendors near the bridge cut the potatoes, fried them in vats of hot oil (some say that it was horse fat and that horse fat makes the best french fry in the world), and sold them on the streets. This humble food—potatoes fried to a crisp—has since taken the world by storm.

More Things to Do with Fries

Bulgarian Fries in Meat and Gravy: True winter fare, these fries are at their best with a paprika-seasoned, very savory sauce and hearty, long-braised meat. Toss the fries in at the last moment and they absorb just enough of the gravy, yet keep their own character. Mmmm.

Chili-Cheese Fries: Now you're talking. Just layer that chili con carne over those fries, and hey, scatter some shredded Cheddar or Jack over the top, too, and give a shake, shake, shake of Tabasco. Yeah!

Chip Butty: Quintessential stick-to-the-ribs fare from the frozen north of England. I'm not necessarily recommending this, merely reporting: Make a sandwich of big fat french fries (chips) inside a buttered roll or two slices of white bread. Serve with HP Sauce (brown sauce).

Indonesian Spicy Fries: Serve your french fries with a generous dollop—as much as you can bear—of oily Chinese/Asian garlic–red chile paste. Use some of the chile mixture and some of the oil. Sizzlingly hot and delish. One of my favorites.

Poutine: Expats from Quebec get teary-eyed thinking about poutine—a mass of hot fries, topped with squeeky cheese curds to melt in and a splash of beefy red wine sauce. I think this might also be an acquired taste.

Shrimp Tempura with Chips: If you're frying up a shrimp tempura, add a potato or two to the menu. Cut into a thin french-fry shape, and fry along with the battered shrimp. Serve with soy dipping sauce, and wasabi or hot chile oil, as well as a vinegar or *yuzu* juice shake on the side.

French Fries

○ ● ○ ● ○ ●

With a french-fried potato, since there are only two ingredients, not counting the salt, the quality and type of these ingredients are of utmost importance, as is technique and temperature. Choose a baking potato, as a waxy potato has a higher sugar content and, when fried, will have a slightly sweet, less desirable, flavor.

As to the oil, controversy reigns over which type to use. Conventional wisdom states that melted suet (beef fat) makes the best french fries, though health concerns and modern practicality point us away from this direction. My favorite oil for frying potatoes is, far and away, olive oil, though it gives the potatoes the definite whiff of southern sunshine. A mild vegetable oil is the oil of choice for much of France these days, but the secret for french fry excellence remains: for the best flavor, melt a piece of beef suet into the oil as it heats through.

There are numerous types of shapes for the fries (always fried twice, the first time to blanch, the second to fry crisply), and each shape contributes to the taste and texture. Thin, thin fries are crisp and crunchy. Thick slices of potatoes are airy and soufflé-like—these big fat potatoes (called, appropriately, Pont Neuf) are my favorite: I love the contrast between the crisp outsides and the very potatoey insides.

Note: A deep-fat thermometer really is a help; without it you can only guess and risk losing the perfection your fries *could* be.

◇ Serves 4 to 6

6 to 8 russets or other baking potatoes
Vegetable or peanut oil, at least 4 to 5 inches deep
Several pieces of beef suet (fat) (optional)
Salt for sprinkling

1 Peel the potatoes (unless you wish to keep a bit of skin; it's not very French, but it's very delicious—the choice is yours) and cut them into one of the following shapes: (1) very thin julienne for shoestring potatoes, (2) 1/4- to 1/2-inch-thick batons for normal to thickish french fries, or (3) 21/2-inch-long, 1/8- to 1/4-inch-thick ovals for *pommes soufflés*.

2 Put the cut potatoes in a large bowl of salted cold water and let them soak for at least an hour, or put in hot tap water and leave for 10 minutes. If you want, you can change the water once or twice during the soaking to remove the extra starch. Drain well and pat dry.

3 In a heavy, deep skillet or a fryer (I use a wok with a stand for stability), heat the oil to a depth of 4 to 5 inches. If using the beef suet, add it to the cold oil and let it melt as the oil heats.

continued

continued

4 Heat the oil to 325°F. Carefully add the potatoes, in small batches if needed to keep the pan from crowding. Fry them for 5 to 10 minutes, stirring them once or twice. They should be almost tender but still very pale and waxy-appearing in color.

5 Lift the fries out of the hot oil using a slotted spoon, and place them on paper towels to drain well. Let the potatoes sit for at least 5 minutes for all the oil to drain off and for the starch to relax a bit.

(For later preparation, arrange the potatoes on a baking sheet and freeze for at least two hours, or until they are frozen. Pack them into plastic freezer bags and freeze for up to two months. You will now have nearly instant homemade french fries when you want.)

6 When ready to serve, reheat the oil to 375°F, and once again, add the potatoes in several batches, cooking them in the bubbling hot oil until they are golden brown, for 5 to 10 minutes. Lift them out of the oil with a slotted spoon and drain them on paper towels. Sprinkle with salt and serve immediately, sizzling hot and fragrant. One of my most enticing french fry experiences was having the crisp fried potatoes served wrapped in a cloth napkin, which kept them warm and grease free.

Variations

Caviar

Use only the best, and lots of it. The salty fishy little nubbins are so tasty on those spuds.

Cilantro Fries

Toss your fries in chopped garlic, cilantro, and thinly sliced green onions, and salt to taste. Add hot sauce and wedges of lemon or lime on the side.

Garlic-Mustard Dip for Fries

Mix 3 tablespoons mild mustard with 1 tablespoon chopped parsley and 1 tablespoon chopped garlic cloves. Dab and dip your fries as desired.

Greek Fries

Available at every souvlaki and gyro joint in Athens, these fries are topped with a mixture of crushed oregano and salt.

Indian-Flavor Fries

Sprinkle fries with your favorite curry powder, or a spice and salt mixture called *chaat*, which is sold in Indian shops. Or sprinkle with aromatic salt and serve with *raita* or *immli*, or both, all from Bollywood Batata Bowl (page 75).

Italian Fries

Garlic fries from New York City. Toss your fries with chopped garlic and parsley.

Spanish Fries

Over your fries, sprinkle a big pinch of Spanish sweet paprika *(pimentón)* mixed with salt, and offer sherry vinegar along with finely chopped fresh tomatoes. For a hit of heat, use hot paprika.

Vinegar

Chips and vinegar: a match made in heaven. Big fat-cut fries, known to all in Blighty as chips, are irresistible; traditionally splashed with malt vinegar and a few shakes of salt, I like the rather refined way of serving french fries of any thickness or thinness with a shower of black truffle vinegar and flaked salt. The vinegar delivers a truffley aroma along with its cargo of mouth-puckering sour; the salt goes *crunch* between your teeth as you bite into the fries. For a party, try serving them wrapped in cones of newspaper.

Charles Phan's
Slanted Door Tomato-Beef Stir-Fry with French Fries!

○ ● ○ ◗ ○ ◗

Charles Phan, chef-owner of San Francisco's legendary Slanted Door restaurant, loved eating french fries tossed into tomato-beef stir-fry when he was growing up in Vietnam. In tomato season, he serves it at his restaurant. When I asked how he makes it, he replied, "Simply toss the fries into tomato-beef stir-fry, in season, of course, when the tomatoes are ripe, sweet, and juicy." This is my version.

◇ Serves 4 as part of a multicourse Asian-style or tapas meal

8 ounces lean beef, thinly sliced into strips for stir-fry

1 tablespoon sweet sherry or rice wine

3 tablespoons dark soy sauce

1½ tablespoons cornstarch

3 tablespoons water

2 tablespoons vegetable oil

1 leek, sliced crosswise about ¼ to ½ inch thick, each slice separated into rings

One 1-inch piece ginger, sliced thinly, then sliced again to make a fine chop

2 garlic cloves, chopped

2 firm tomatoes, cut into wedges

½ cup vegetable, chicken, or beef broth

½ recipe French Fries (page 133)

Sea salt for sprinkling

3 tablespoons chopped cilantro

1 In a small bowl, mix the beef strips with the sherry and soy sauce, and set aside. In a separate bowl, mix the cornstarch with the water and set aside.

2 Heat a wok or heavy skillet, then pour in 1 tablespoon of the vegetable oil. Stir-fry the leek, ginger, and garlic for a moment, or long enough to soften. Off heat, remove the mixture from the wok, leaving behind the oil, and add more as needed. Return the wok to the heat, and quickly stir-fry the tomato wedges only until they slightly char in places. Do not cook too much; you do not want sauce. Transfer to the plate with the leek, ginger, and garlic.

3 Return the wok to the stove, and when hot and smoking, use a slotted spoon to remove the beef from its marinade (reserving the marinade for the sauce) and stir-fry for a moment in the hot wok. Cook it for a minute or so, stir-frying, then transfer from the wok to the plate with the vegetables. Add the broth to the wok, and when it starts to boil, remove from the heat and add the cornstarch and the soy sauce marinade reserved from the meat. The sauce will thicken.

4 Return the vegetables, meat, and juices to the wok, toss together, then toss in the french fries. Heat through and serve right away, sprinkled with a little sea salt and the cilantro.

Kathleen's Potatoes
with Rosemary, Bacon, and Duck Fat

○ ● ○ ◗ ○ ●

If you've lost the will to live, these potatoes will revive you, body and soul! When I asked Kathleen McElroy, then *New York Times* Dining In editor, about her fave potato dish, her face lit up with potato-love and she exclaimed, "Rosemary . . . duck fat . . . *and* bacon!" "All that in one pan?" I asked. Then I went home, fried it up, and sat at the table forking up these blissful potatoes, thinking they were just perfect, the most delicious things I'd ever eaten. These potatoes are culinary miracle workers, lifting the darkest depression and brightening any mood. I feel an inner smile just thinking about them.

◇ Serves 4 as a side dish, 2 as a main dish

4 ounces lardons (diced meaty, lean bacon)

3 tablespoons duck or goose fat, as needed

2 pounds potatoes, peeled and sliced about ⅛ inch thick

1 tablespoon chopped fresh rosemary, as needed

Coarse or flaked salt and coarsely ground black pepper

1 In a heavy skillet, preferably nonstick, lightly brown the lardons until they are browned in spots but still quite succulent. Push them to one side of the pan.

2 Heat a tablespoon of the duck fat over medium-high heat and add a layer of the sliced potatoes, fitting them in, and cooking them until they seem lightly browned in places and they start to turn soft and slightly translucent.

3 With a spatula, push the potatoes over to one side, picking up as much of the bacon as you can when you gather up the potatoes. Bits of bacon are going to fall in between the potatoes as you keep adding potatoes and turning them; the bacon will brown and crisp anyhow without your doing anything about it.

4 Make another layer of potatoes, and continue to cook, lowering the heat slightly if needed. Sprinkle with rosemary, salt, and pepper, and continue this way, pushing the potatoes over to one pile on the side of the pan, turning the potatoes, adding more duck fat as you do, and more rosemary, salt, and pepper.

5 When all the potatoes have turned into a golden and golden-brown pile of potatoes and smell divine, it's time to serve.

Rockin' Fried Potatoes
with Wild Citrus Mojo Sauce

This is just potatoes and olive oil, a sprinkling of salt, and a Mojo Sauce, though you could serve it with a scattering of chopped parsley and garlic. The thing that sets this fried potato recipe against the others is the way the potatoes are prepared: boiled first whole in their skins, then held in a cloth and gently squeezed and crushed. You end up with a flat, thick patty that kind of falls apart when it hits the hot oil. It browns in a most interesting way, and all the tiny lumps and bumps, as well as the skin, are browned and crisped deliciously. Use waxy potatoes, such as Ruby Gold, a waxy Yukon-type golden potato with a red skin; ordinary red potatoes may also be used.

Mojo, by the way, is simply a sexy word for a spicy vinaigrette from the Caribbean. This Mojo Sauce is probably nowhere near authentic, but never mind, it's so darned tasty. You might find yourself splashing it onto lamb or sausages at a barbecue, or using it as a sauce for roasted chicken. You can use whichever citrus you like, though you should have at least some lime juice or lemon; other than that, you could include grapefruit, orange, or mandarin; and if you don't feel like making Mojo Sauce, never mind—I don't frown at either plain old vinegar, a shake of hot sauce, or even . . . ketchup . . . for these terrific potatoes.

◇ Serves 4 to 6

6 large waxy potatoes, such as Ruby Gold, whole and unpeeled

Olive oil for frying

Coarse salt for sprinkling

Fresh chopped parsley or cilantro, hot sauce of choice, and chopped onions (optional)

Mojo Sauce (optional) (recipe follows)

1 Place the potatoes in a saucepan with water to cover. Bring to a boil, then lower the heat to a gentle rolling boil and cook until just tender. This will depend on the size and age of the potatoes; test by using a sharp paring knife or skewer. Do not overcook as they will fall apart. Pour off the water and set aside.

2 When cool enough to handle, place the potatoes, one by one, in a clean towel and, holding tightly with your hands, gently apply pressure until you hear and feel the potato flatten. Continue crushing evenly so that you have a big thick flattish potato that is slightly broken in many spots. You want to keep them together as much as possible, though they will come apart in all different places when they hit the hot oil.

3 Heat 2 inches of the olive oil in a heavy skillet until smoking, then gently slide in each potato. Keep the heat high and brown the potatoes on each side until quite brown. Transfer to a paper towel to drain. They may be reheated if not serving right away.

4 Serve with parsley, hot sauce, and onions, or Mojo Sauce, if desired.

Variations
Aloo Makallah

A favorite dish of the long-ago Calcutta Jewish community. Blanch very small peeled potatoes (or cut large potatoes into bite-size chunks) in turmeric water to turn the water golden, add enough salt to give the water flavor. When the potatoes are almost ready, after 6 to 8 minutes, drain gently and let cool. Fry as directed until browned and crusty.

Mojo Sauce

3 tablespoons extra-virgin olive oil

10 garlic cloves, thinly sliced

1/3 cup orange or mandarin juice

2 tablespoons Key lime, Mexican *limón*, or other fresh, lively lime juice

1/2 teaspoon cumin

Salt and black pepper

In a saucepan, heat the olive oil over low heat with the garlic until the garlic softens and turns golden but does not brown. Add the orange juice, lime juice, and cumin, and cook over high heat for 2 to 3 minutes or until it condenses but doesn't evaporate and burn. If it threatens to do this, add a little water or more citrus juice. Season to taste with salt and pepper.

Thin Wafers of Fried Potato
with Preserved Lemon, Garlic,
and Saffron Aioli

These french fries are inspired by the *pommes frites* I've been running into lately, such as at San Francisco's Medjool in the Mission District and Lluna Basque in North Beach; thin, crisp, flat little almost-noodles of fried potatoes, instead of the more usual fat, evenly cut french fries. The aioli is optional, though rich—there is nothing quite like a slick of its garlicky presence on a fluffy little pile of crisp fries. If you're not in the mood for thin shreds of preserved lemon, scatter a handful of chopped herbs plus a shot of wine vinegar. Or try a North African spice mixture of cumin, paprika, and cayenne, with some flakes of salt. Or bottled hot sauce and a squirt of lime juice. Or Black Olive–Rosemary Aioli.

◇ Serves 4 to 6

1½ pounds russets or other baking potatoes, peeled

Vegetable oil, or half vegetable oil and half olive oil, for frying

2 garlic cloves, chopped

1 to 2 Moroccan preserved lemons, the flesh removed and discarded, the peel rinsed and finely chopped or 3 tablespoons chopped fresh herbs of choice, such as parsley, oregano, chives, chervil, or cilantro

Wine vinegar, for sprinkling

Black Olive–Rosemary Aioli (page 44)

Saffron Aioli (page 142)

1 Cut each potato lengthwise into 3 or 4 pieces, then cut or feed through the slicer of the food processor so that you get thin, rectangular flat shapes, almost noodle-like. Place in cold water to soak for up to 2 hours.

2 Drain and place on paper towels, in several batches, to dry.

3 Heat a wok or skillet filled with several inches of oil. When the oil is hot enough to smoke, gently add about a third of the potatoes, spread into a single layer, and fry sizzling in the hot oil. The first batch will be a precooking batch; do not let them get too crisp. When they just soften, remove from the oil and drain on paper towels. Repeat until all the potatoes are done.

4 Just before serving, reheat the oil, adding more if needed for a depth of several inches. When it is smoking, gently add about a third of the potatoes to the hot oil, fry and sizzle, then turn and cook the other side. Remove from the pan and drain on

continued

continued

paper towels. Place on a baking sheet and keep warm. Repeat until all the potatoes are cooked until crisp.

5 Serve the hot *frites* with a sprinkling of the garlic, then a choice of either chopped preserved lemon or chopped fresh herbs. Offer your favorite vinegar and aioli, if desired, alongside.

Saffron Aioli

1 generous pinch saffron threads, about 10

1 garlic clove, crushed with a pinch or two of salt

1 egg yolk

½ teaspoon mustard of choice

Juice of ¼ lemon, or more

½ cup olive oil or vegetable oil, or a combination

Pinch of cayenne pepper, or drop of Tabasco sauce

1 Crush the saffron in a mortar and pestle, then add the garlic and salt and crush it together with the saffron.

2 Add this paste to the food processor with the egg yolk, mustard, and lemon juice. With the motor running, slowly add the olive oil, a few spoonfuls at a time, until it thickens. Then with the motor still running, pour the rest in steadily in a thin stream, adding more as the sauce thickens and looks ready to absorb more oil. To do this in a bowl, whisk the saffron-garlic paste with the egg yolk, mustard, and lemon juice, then slowly beat in, a spoonful or two at a time, the olive oil, beating until the mixture absorbs the oil, then adding a tiny bit more in a thin, steady stream.

3 Season to taste with cayenne pepper. Chill until ready to serve.

Pommes de Terre à l'Ail

Pan-Browned Potatoes with Garlic and Parsley

○ ◐ ○ ◑ ○ ●

This is a classic bistro dish, eaten in varying guises throughout France, especially in the Jura, the Dordogne, or old-fashioned traditional Parisian bistros. The crisp pan-browned potatoes are tossed with garlic and parsley at the end, which gives fresh spunky flavor and aroma, rather than cooking together with the potatoes. The dish is blissfully delicious with roast duck or chicken, and especially with grilled steak béarnaise.

The choice of fat is yours in this dish; whichever you choose will give its character to the potatoes. You could make it different each time and enjoy it all the more for the variety.

◇ Serves 4

1 pound small, waxy new potatoes

Salt

4 tablespoons butter, olive oil, or duck or goose fat

Black pepper

3 garlic cloves, finely chopped

¹/₂ bunch parsley, chervil, or chives, or a combination, finely chopped

1 Place the potatoes in a saucepan with water to cover. Add a pinch of salt, then bring the potatoes to a boil. Cook for a minute or two, then remove from the heat and cover. Leave to cool in the water, then drain. Rinse in cold water and peel; either use now or chill until ready to use, up to three days.

2 Slice the potatoes ¹/₄ to ¹/₂ inch thick.

3 In a heavy nonstick skillet, heat about half the butter over medium-high heat. Make a single layer of the sliced potatoes, sprinkle to taste with salt and pepper, and sauté until they are crispy browned at the edges; turn the potatoes over and pile them up on the side of the pan, then add another single layer of potatoes, brown, and pile these up with the other potatoes, tossing and turning them, letting them all brown evenly as you go, sprinkling with salt and pepper every so often and adding the rest of the fat. Repeat until many of the potatoes are golden and crisp around the edges and all are cooked through.

4 Serve sizzling hot, sprinkled with the chopped garlic and parsley.

Variation
Pommes de Terres de la Mère

A French mamma's potatoes, pan browned with a vinegar-cream sauce, eat it with any rich winey meat, grilled duck, steak, or fish. Prepare as directed, then remove the potatoes from the pan and blot on paper towels; keep warm. Pour off the fat in the pan, then add about 2 tablespoons wine vinegar and cook it down for a few minutes to take off its sour edge. Add a cup of cream, and heat through. Serve hot sprinkled with a tablespoon or two of parsley, chervil, or chives.

Latkes

Eastern European Jewish Potato Pancakes

○ ● ○ ● ○ ●

A latke is simply a pancake of shredded or grated raw potatoes mixed with onion, bound together with a bit of egg, and flour or matzo meal or both, then fried until golden brown and crisp. But it has iconic value and never tastes simply like a potato pancake—a latke tastes like a latke!

I'd like to claim the title of Latke Queen, but alas, I know that there are too many out there who would fight me bare-handed to wear that crown instead. When it comes to latkes, there is no such thing as fair play: your own latkes taste best and that's all there is to it. Put another way, there is much variation, and most are really, really good. But the flavor of your very own latke will taste of your very own childhood, and that will taste best of all.

Probably my friend Etty is a true Latke Queen. All year long she cooks nothing (not quite nothing; she will make a brilliant if occasional schnitzel). Her husband owns a deli; why should she cook? But when Chanukah comes along, Etty gets out her potatoes and the frying commences. Possibly, I would relinquish my crown to her. On the other hand, twin crowns to my Auntie Sarah and Auntie Ella, who make big batches of latkes and keep them in their freezer for serving anytime. An invitation to an auntie's house for dinner is "anytime," and whenever that might be, the chicken will be surrounded by latkes and all eaters around the table will be wearing smiles.

But the most honestly earned crown of all must go to my friend Esther, who once volunteered to help me make 400 latkes, in her kitchen. We filled box after box after box with crisp browned potato pancakes; and since oil-scented perfumes wafted their way around her kitchen, by the end of the evening, the walls needed repainting.

6 medium-large baking potatoes

2 eggs

2 onions

1½ teaspoons salt

Small pinch of sugar

¼ cup flour

¼ cup matzo meal

½ teaspoon baking powder

Vegetable oil, or olive oil, for frying

Sour cream or Greek yogurt

Applesauce (homemade or from a jar)

Chunky Applesauce with Cranberries (recipe follows)

Beet and Onion Marmalade (page 146)

Sour Cream and Lox (page 146)

1 Peel the potatoes if you wish; if you don't wish to, just scrub them and resolve yourself to some shreds of skin in the pancakes.

2 Shred the potatoes over the large holes of a grater or a food processor. Place the shredded potatoes in a bowl and cover with cold water. Set aside.

3 Beat the eggs lightly. Grate the onions over the large holes of a grater into the eggs, then stir in the salt, sugar, flour, matzo meal, and baking powder.

4 Drain the potatoes very well, then place in a clean cloth and squeeze as dry as you can. Place half the potatoes in the food processor and whirl until they are finely chopped or puréed.

5 Add both the shredded and puréed potatoes to the egg mixture, and stir well.

6 In a heavy nonstick skillet, heat about ½ inch oil over medium-high heat; when the oil is hot but not yet smoking, it is ready. A good way to test it is to drop a bread cube in; if it sizzles and browns nicely fairly quickly, the oil is ready.

7 Drop heaping tablespoons of the potato mixture into the hot oil. Press down on each blob of potato mixture as the bottom cooks, so that the pancake flattens and thins, browning better. When the bottom is golden brown and crisp, turn over and repeat; try not to turn too many times or the latkes will get a bit heavy. If you are going to be using the batter later, add a little vitamin C to the batter, cover tight with plastic wrap, and refrigerate until ready to use. (Half of a vitamin C tablet, crushed, keeps the potatoes from turning brown the same way a squirt of lemon juice does a sliced apple.)

8 Remove the latkes from the pan and drain on paper towels.

9 Serve at once with sour cream and applesauce, or choose one of the following toppings.

Toppings

Chunky Applesauce with Cranberries: Dice 5 tart green apples (I don't bother peeling), and put in a saucepan with the juice and zest of ½ lemon, 1 cinnamon stick, and ½ cup sugar. Cover tightly and cook over medium heat until the apples give off some of their liquid and soften, for about 15 minutes. If the apples threaten to scorch or burn, add a little bit of water or apple juice. When the apple chunks are tender, add a 12-ounce bag of cranberries, and return to the stove, covered, for 8 more minutes or so, just long enough for the berries to pop but not fall apart into mush. Refrigerate.

continued

continued

Beet and Onion Marmalade: Stew diced beets with thinly sliced onions, sugar to taste, a large pinch of allspice, and a splash of vinegar, until it's all tender and jamlike. Serve a dab on top of latkes with either a dollop of sour cream or a slice of foie gras.

Sour Cream and Lox: Eat latkes topped with a dollop of sour cream and a slice or two of smoked salmon (lox). Sprinkle with chives. A dab of briny caviar is delish, too.

Variations

Dr. Esther's Father's Buttery Kugel

A kugel is a pudding, or rather a mixture of soft ingredients, poured into a casserole pan and baked, rather than made into pancakes, as in these latkes-turned-kugel. Some people use chicken fat, others—myself included—olive oil, while the best kugel in the world was made by my friend Dr. Esther's father, Harry Novak, an Eastern European Jew turned American cowboy, who melted a stick of butter into the hot pan and then poured the potato batter in and baked it. The kugel tasted like buttery potatoey goodness. I always remember Esther's father so warmly when I think of these potatoes.

Prepare the potato batter as directed. Heat a baking pan (9 x 12 inches approximately, or large enough to hold the batter) in a hot, say 400°F, oven, with 4 to 6 tablespoons fat until the fat is almost smoking. Pour the potato batter into the hot fat and smooth it flat, then return to the oven. Reduce heat to 350°F to 375°F and bake for about an hour, or just long enough for the top to go crusty browned and the inside to stay creamy and moist. A kugel is delicious sliced up the next day as a snack or as an accompaniment to any meal.

Latkes but Not Latkes

Only potatoes and onions—some swear by latkes that have no egg, flour, or matzo meal. To be perfectly honest, this variation are lovely fried shredded potato cakes, but they are *not* latkes. Proceed as directed, shredding both potatoes and onions on the shredder. Place the mixture in a clean towel and twist the bottom to squeeze out all the liquid. Place the shredded and dried potatoes and onions in a bowl. Season with salt, pepper, and a pinch of sugar, then fry in heaped tablespoons in about 1/4 inch or so of hot oil. When golden brown and crisp on the first side, turn. They will be quite thin and very potatoey.

Asian-Flavor Potato Pancakes

To the flourless and eggless potato pancake batter above, add a shake of red pepper flakes along with several chopped garlic cloves. Serve the fried pancakes with stir-fried Asian greens that you have made zippier with a spoonful of fermented hot bean sauce or hot bean oil.

Vietnamese Prawn and Potato Pancakes

Shred the potatoes only; do not blend into a purée. Add 1 pound prawns; if large, cut into small pieces. Serve the fried pancakes with Thai basil and mint or cilantro, lettuce leaves to wrap the pancakes in, and Vietnamese dipping sauce (combine 4 tablespoons lime juice with 2 tablespoons fish sauce, 2 tablespoons water, 1 teaspoon brown sugar, 1/2 teaspoon salt, and 1/2 to 1 fresh small red chile, cut into thin slices) for dunking.

Persian Saffron-Dill Pilaf
with a Crisp Potato Crust

○ ● ○ ● ○ ●

The classic Persian way of making pilaf is to partially cook the rice, then drain and rinse it well
to rid it of excess starch and produce a light grain. Handfuls are then sprinkled into the bottom of a hot
pan, in melted butter, then the remaining rice is added to the top, the pot is covered with a clean
cloth, and a lid is added. It's cooked over a very low heat, with several dabs of butter added to the top, and
whatever spices or other ingredients are being used: braised lamb, garden herbs, sautéed vegetables.
The pilaf steams slowly and is then served up, the bottom layer a crisp crunchy disk,
broken up so that everyone gets a piece of it to contrast with the tender rice. This crunchy layer is
called *tah dig*; mention it to any Persian and he will get a dreamy look in his eyes, if he is a *tah
dig* lover, that is. And Persians who are lovers of the finest *tah dig* ever, sliced potato *tah dig*
(in my humble opinion), will probably get out a pan and start assembling the ingredients—that's
how excited everyone gets at first thought of this dish.

Here is why: Your rice cooks over a layer of thinly sliced browned potatoes. The potatoes
absorb the flavors and butteriness of the rice, and the contrast of crisp and creamy potato with soft,
fragrant rice is sumptuous. Serve with any braised Middle Eastern dish or with savory grilled kebabs,
accompanied by a bowl of yogurt and a plate of cucumbers and sprigs of fresh herbs,
such as dill, tarragon, green onions, mint, cilantro, or parsley.

◇ Serves 4 to 6

1 cup long-grain rice

4 to 6 tablespoons unsalted butter

1 large or 1½ medium russet potatoes, peeled and very
thinly sliced

2 to 3 large pinches of saffron threads

Salt as desired

2 tablespoons coarsely chopped fresh dill

continued

continued

1 Bring a large saucepan filled with water to a boil; add the rice and boil for about 5 minutes, or until the rice kernels are not quite cooked through: bite into one—the core of the grain should be a little crunchy. Drain and rinse in cold water, then drain again. Set aside.

2 In a wide-bottomed, heavy nonstick saucepan, heat about half the butter. Working in one layer at a time, lightly sauté the potato slices, removing each layer as it is cooked through.

3 When all the potato slices are tender, arrange the layers on the bottom of the saucepan, going up the sides about a quarter of the way. Sprinkle with a pinch of saffron and salt, then add about a third of the rice, dab with about a third of the remaining butter, then a sprinkling of saffron and dill. Repeat with rice, saffron, salt, dill, and butter, ending with butter.

4 Cover the top of the saucepan tightly with a clean cloth, then place a heavy, tight-fitting lid on top of that.

5 Heat over medium-low heat, without disturbing the rice, and cook gently, letting the potatoes brown a bit and the rice finish cooking in its own steam, for about 10 minutes. Do not let the potatoes burn.

6 Remove from the heat and let sit for a further 10 minutes or so. Unmold onto a platter. If the potato *tah dig* comes out easily in one disk, that is wonderful; if it doesn't, that is fine, too—simply cut the potato crust into pieces and serve along with the rice.

Potatoes for

Meat and Potatoes, Fish and Potatoes, Potatoes and Potatoes! The truth is, many people don't even consider it dinner unless there are potatoes.

Some might serve the main course with a big side dish of potatoes. Mashed potatoes are made for this; gratin, *mais oui*! French fries? But, of course.

But then there are the dishes that are as much about potatoes as they are about the main event: chunks of potatoes simmered into stews, a huge mound of potatoes beneath a braised lamb shank, tomatoey potatoes with the scent of the sea. As the potatoes cook, they are perfumed with the flavors and aromas of the other ingredients in the pot.

And tell me, which of us doesn't search through the plate, in between enjoying the morsel of meat, the chunk of vegetable, the spoonful of savory sauce . . . which of us isn't hunting for that bit of potato? The potatoes are always the parts that are eaten up first, never left behind. At least in my house.

Dinner!

Dinners to Add Potatoes To

Goulash: Stewed beef, veal, or pork, with paprika, peppers, and tomatoes, and an almost equal amount of potato chunks or quarters, is your basic goulash. Yum.

Greek Dishes: Greeks add cut-up peeled potatoes to almost any meat, fish, or poultry, season well, splash with olive oil, and add water to cover, then braise slowly to succulent tenderness. The potatoes pick up the flavor of whatever they are cooked with. Take the cover off for the final 20 or 30 minutes of cooking to brown and intensify the juices a bit.

Malaysian and Thai Curries: Rich coconut curries are usually enriched with a handful of small waxy potatoes. Use creamers, fingerlings, Jersey Royals, or if you are lucky, any of the really succulent potatoes such as the Malaysian Peruvian ones (known as Inca Gold in the U.K.).

Meaty Stews: Peel large floury potatoes and cut into quarters or halves. About an hour before the braising dish is done, add the potatoes to a brisket with carrots, Jewish style; roasting lamb, Greek style; or a winey braise, French style. Bake until the potatoes are just tender.

Moussaka: For a moussaka using 1 to 1$\frac{1}{2}$ pounds ground meat (either with or without eggplant), cut potatoes into $\frac{1}{2}$-inch pieces and gently cook the potatoes in a skillet in a few tablespoons of extra-virgin olive oil. Layer and proceed as with any moussaka.

Pasta con le Patate
Pasta with Potatoes, Tomatoes, and Cheese, from Old Napoli

○ ● ○ ● ○ ●

Mamma mia! Pasta with potatoes, both in a bowl, slapped all around with diced tomatoes
and melty cheese? How excessively delicious are we? Very.

Serving pasta with a potato sauce is traditional in old Napoli, and I for one love it.
My favorite Pasta con le Patate is made at Europeo restaurant in Napoli, a friendly atmospheric
trattoria that makes traditional dishes so luscious you could just cry.

◇ Serves 4 to 6

6 tablespoons extra-virgin olive oil

1 leek, trimmed and thinly sliced

2 to 3 waxy potatoes (about 10 ounces), peeled and cut
into ½-inch dice

4 garlic cloves, coarsely chopped

3 large ripe fresh tomatoes, diced

3 cups chicken or vegetable broth

1 to 2 tablespoons chopped fresh rosemary leaves

1 cup canned diced tomatoes

2 tablespoons tomato paste

12 ounces seashell pasta

10 ounces cheese, such as Jack or provolone

2 tablespoons thinly sliced fresh basil

Cheese for grating, such as Parmesan, Grana Padano,
pecorino, or Asiago

1 In a large, heavy nonstick skillet, heat the olive oil over
medium-high heat, and lightly sauté the leek and potatoes.
When the leek is soft and the potatoes begin to turn translucent,
add the garlic, fresh tomatoes, chicken broth, rosemary, and
canned tomatoes. Bring to a boil, then reduce the heat, and
cook for about 10 minutes.

2 Stir in the tomato paste, then add the pasta. Continue to boil
until the pasta is cooked through, for about 20 minutes.

3 Add the 10 ounces of cheese, tossing to combine, over the
heat, so that the cheese melts. Sprinkle with basil and serve
right away, with grated cheese.

Kim's Carnitas
with Potatoes

○ ● ○ ◗ ○ ●

My buddy Kim—that is, the respected food writer Kim Severson—made a sweep of New York's
Union Square Greenmarket, snatched up some gorgeous pork—both fresh and smoked—
and tossed it in a big pan for carnitas with potatoes. In the mood, I followed in her cooking shoes but had
only turkey in my kitchen, and some delectable nuggets of lean bacon. Since I was in big-time potato-mode
I jumped into the cooking, anyway. The result is right here: chunks of crisp, tender turkey and bacon,
and morsels of potatoes, all mingled together with each other's juices. Delish! If you want to
use smoked turkey instead of bacon, go right ahead, but don't use the leg as it has small bones
and cartilage that needs to be picked away before eating.

◇ Serves 4

1 pound pork belly, breast, shoulder, or leg, or turkey breast, or breast and thigh chunks, cut into 1- to 2-bite morsels

4 ounces very lean bacon, or smoked pork, cut into nuggets, lardon style

1 onion, chopped

½ green bell pepper, chopped

2 bay leaves

2 cups broth, or enough just to cover

½ teaspoon oregano leaves, crushed between your hands

1 teaspoon cumin seeds

1 teaspoon mild red chili powder, such as New Mexican or Californian

12 ounces slightly waxy potatoes, peeled and cut into chunks about 2 x 3 inches in size, or as desired

2 garlic cloves, thinly sliced

2 to 3 tablespoons olive oil or duck fat, if the bacon is lean

1 Place the pork or turkey, bacon, onion, bell pepper, and bay leaves in a heavy nonstick skillet, then pour in the broth and sprinkle in the oregano, cumin seeds, and chili powder. Over medium-high heat, bring to a boil. Reduce the heat and simmer until the meat is very tender, for about 35 minutes for pork, or for about 15 minutes for turkey.

2 Add the potatoes and garlic, then raise the heat, turning the potatoes once or twice for them to cook evenly but not turn to mush.

3 The potatoes should be cooked through when the liquid has just about evaporated. If there is no fat in the pan, add the olive oil and cook, letting the meat and potatoes brown, turning every so often.

4 When the meat and potatoes are slightly browned, and surrounded with a delicious sludgey spicy mixture, it is ready. Serve right away.

The Mushroom Forager's
Cottage Pie

Almost everyone loves a casserole of savory meat topped with a layer of mashed potatoes; call it cottage pie (when it's made with beef), call it shepherd's pie (when it's made with lamb). The French call it Hachis Parmentier, a hash in honor of the man who brought France potatoes: Antoine-Auguste Parmentier. Because this is prepared with beef, it is technically a cottage pie, but because it is so full of mushrooms, it seems that the cottage must belong to a mushroom forager.

Anyhow, back to the pie. I like to make this wide and thin as the flavors have a certain elegance . . . and it is lovely made individually—not only does it look rather festive, but you have more edges to get crisp, and it's tidy on your plate rather than sloppily served. Use individual ramekins, or use the round molds that are used in restaurants, place them on a baking sheet and layer the meat and potatoes in. Bake, then remove each with a spatula, cut around the edge to loosen the mold, and remove. The pie should stay on the plate, and look very fetching.

But even if your Mushroom Forager's Cottage Pie serves up sloppily, I think that you'll be glad—very, very glad—that you decided to make it.

◇ Serves 4

5 medium-size white potatoes, either floury or waxy, peeled and cut into chunks

Salt

1/2 to 3/4 ounce dried porcini mushrooms

1 dried shiitake, or Chinese black mushroom, stem removed

2 cups vegetable, beef, or chicken broth

3 garlic cloves, thinly sliced

A grating of nutmeg

1 tablespoon olive oil, or as needed

1 onion, chopped

1 pound lean ground beef

A few generous shakes of soy sauce

4 to 6 tablespoons sour cream

4 tablespoons butter

3 tablespoons low-fat milk, or as needed

continued

continued

1 Place the potatoes in a saucepan with salted water to cover. Bring to a boil, reduce the heat to medium, and cook until they are just tender, then drain. This can be done up to two days ahead of time.

2 Place the porcini and shiitake mushrooms in a saucepan with the broth to cover. Bring to a boil, then reduce the heat, and cook, uncovered, until the mushrooms are very rehydrated. Let boil for 5 to 10 minutes to reduce the volume of liquid and intensify the flavor. Add the garlic and nutmeg, and remove from the heat to cool. This can be done up to two days ahead of time and kept in the refrigerator.

3 In a heavy nonstick skillet, heat the olive oil over medium heat, then add the onion and beef, and cook, stirring and breaking up the meat, until the onion is limp and the meat is browned in spots.

4 Mash up about 2 potatoes worth of potato and add it to the pan. Pour off the liquid from the mushrooms, then chop the rehydrated mushrooms and add those to the skillet with the meat sauce. Cook over high heat until the liquid has almost evaporated and the whole is savory and delicious. Remove from the heat, stir in the soy sauce, mixing well, then the sour cream. This can be done up to two days ahead of time and kept in the refrigerator.

5 Preheat the oven to 400°F. Make a layer of the meat mixture in the bottom of a 9-inch pie or cake pan. I like round, but an oval, square, or rectangle pan is fine, too. Mash the remaining potatoes with 3 tablespoons of the butter and the milk. Spread on top of the meat mixture, and cut the remaining tablespoon of butter into bits, then poke the bits into the top of the potato layer.

6 Bake for about 25 minutes, or until the top is golden in spots and lightly browned around the edges.

7 Eat right away.

Roesti
Swiss Buttery Shredded Potato Cake

○ ● ○ ● ○ ●

The secret to delectable roesti is using potatoes that have been cooked long enough to stabilize their starch but not so long as to go mushy. You can use potatoes that you have boiled ahead of time, up to a week. They are simply shredded potatoes and butter, lots of lovely butter, crisp edges of potato on the outside, smooshy, rich, creamy potato shreds within—sublime.

Then again, you can add shredded cheese, and these roesti are very yummy in a different way. Or a handful of chopped herbs added to the potatoes: same thing, very herby roesti. You can use roesti as a base to serve up something else on top, say, mushrooms in a sour cream stroganoff-y sauce, or stir-fried strips of meat in a mustard cream sauce.

◇ Serves 4

8 medium-size Yukon Gold or russet potatoes (1½ to 2 pounds), whole and unpeeled

4 to 6 tablespoons butter, or a combination of butter and oil, more as needed

Salt and freshly ground black pepper

1 to 2 tablespoons chopped garlic and chopped fresh herbs, such as chives, chervil, or parsley (optional)

1 Place the potatoes in a saucepan with water to cover. Bring to a boil; reduce the heat to medium-high, and cook until the potatoes are cooked halfway through, that is, your knife or fork can penetrate them a bit but then they get crunchy. Remove the potatoes from the heat, drain, and set aside. If you have a stash of already cooked potatoes, you're halfway to your roesti. Omit this boiling step.

2 When cool enough to handle, shred the potatoes over the largest holes of your shredder, or use your food processor. Discard as much of the skin as you can after shredding.

3 Preheat the oven to 375°F. Heat a large, heavy nonstick skillet and add about a third of the butter. Spoon in about a quarter of the potatoes, and press with your spoon or spatula to flatten them into a big flat cake. Dot with butter, sprinkle with salt and pepper, and repeat the layering, saving the last quarter or so of the butter to dot on top of the potatoes when you roast them. Flatten lightly as you make the layers.

4 Cook the potato cake on the stove over medium heat, letting the bottom turn golden and crisp. After about 10 to 15 minutes, dot with the remaining butter, place in the oven, and continue to roast until the top is golden brown, for about 25 to 30 minutes. The longer you bake it, the thicker and crisper the crust will be. As long as you don't burn it, it will be delish.

5 Sprinkle the roesti with garlic and herbs (if using) and serve right away.

Variation
Cheese Roesti

Gently toss the shredded potatoes with about 10 ounces shredded cheese, such as Cheddar with its butterfat content and nice strong flavor, and toss in 4 to 5 thinly sliced green onions, too, then proceed as in the main recipe, cutting the butter way back to 2 or 3 tablespoons (as the butterfat of the cheese will help crisp the potatoes). Serve with a mixture of baby lettuces, such as wild arugula, purslane, chives, baby romaine, mâche, and watercress, dressed with a tangy vinaigrette.

Enchiladas de Patatas

Potato Enchiladas with Red Chile Sauce and Melty Cheese

○ ● ○ ● ○ ●

Mmmmmm, *muy delicioso!* There's only one thing better than enchiladas, and that is *potato* enchiladas! Fragrant with cilantro, rich with melty cheese, and splashed with a bright chile sauce. They're delicious at all hours. Eat 'em topped with an egg and salsa for an any-time-of-the-day-or-night breakfast.

◇ Serves 4

12 ounces potatoes, either floury or all-purpose, meaning somewhere in the middle between floury and waxy

Salt

3 tablespoons olive oil or other cooking fat, or as needed

1 onion, chopped

2 garlic cloves, chopped

4 tablespoons mild chile powder, such as ancho, New Mexican, or California, or a combination of fragrant mild chile powders

2 cups water, broth, or half water and half broth

Large pinch of oregano leaves, crumbled in your hands

Large pinch—($1/8$ to $1/4$ teaspoon)—of cumin

Juice of $1/2$ lime

$1/4$ to $1/2$ teaspoon garlic powder

6 green onions, thinly sliced

2 tablespoons chopped cilantro

12 ounces fresh cheese, such as *queso fresco* or Monterey Jack, diced or crumbled

2 ounces sharp pungent cheese, such as *queso anejo*, dried Jack, aged pecorino, Parmesan, or Grana Padano

12 corn tortillas

8 to 12 ounces mature Cheddar or creamy Jack, grated, for melting on top of the enchiladas

$1/2$ head romaine lettuce, thinly sliced or shredded (about $1 1/2$ to 2 cups)

Sour cream, for topping enchiladas

10 to 12 radishes, thinly sliced

$1/4$ cup pickled jalapeños

1 Cook the potatoes in gently boiling salted water to cover, until they are just tender; this will depend upon the type, size, and age of the potatoes. Drain and set aside. When they are cool enough to handle, using a clean dish towel, hold on to each potato and peel, then dice. Set aside.

2 In a large, heavy nonstick skillet, heat 2 tablespoons of the olive oil over medium-high heat, and lightly sauté the onion and garlic until softened, for about 5 minutes, then sprinkle in the chile powder, cook a moment or so, and pour in the water. Bring to a boil, then reduce the heat and simmer for about 5 minutes further. Season with oregano, cumin, lime juice, and garlic powder, and remove from the heat.

3 Combine the diced potatoes with the green onions, cilantro, about one-third of the fresh cheese, and one-third of the pungent cheese. Set aside.

4 Preheat the oven to 375°F to 400°F.

5 In a heavy, preferably nonstick skillet, warm the tortillas in the remaining oil. As each tortilla becomes pliable from the heat of the pan, place it on a plate and arrange a tablespoon or two of the filling along one side of the tortilla (you will have filling left for saucing the tortillas). Roll up or fold, and arrange the filled tortilla in a baking pan in a single layer. Repeat until all the tortillas have been filled.

6 Pour the reserved sauce over the top, sprinkle with the reserved cheese, and bake until the cheese melts, the edges of the tortillas are crispy, and the whole is heated through, for about 20 minutes.

7 Serve right away, garnished with the lettuce, sour cream, radishes, and pickled jalapeños.

Bacalao con Papas
Salt Cod and Potatoes Stewed with Chorizo and Tomatoes

○ ● ○ ● ○ ●

Adding parboiled waxy potatoes to the savory tomatoey sauce for the *bacalao* (salt cod)
keeps the starch inside the potatoes and keeps the sauce clear instead of thick and potatoey—
though there are times when thick and potatoey is what you want. Mild-fleshed cod is a delicious partner
with chorizo—classic Spanish fare—so if you can't find salt cod or don't want to worry about soaking it,
use fresh. You could, for more of a cioppino flavor, make this with clams or other seafood instead of the
salt cod, or no fish at all: add a big handful of peas for a garden rather than seaside flavor.

Serve this dish with rustic sourdough country bread and extra olive oil for drizzling, and start
with a tapa of feta sprinkled with oregano, roasted red bell pepper warmed with garlic,
and cool refreshing cucumbers.

◇ Serves 4 to 6

8 to 10 ounces salt cod, or an equal amount of fresh cod

10 to 12 ounces small waxy new potatoes

Salt

1 head of garlic, cloves peeled and thinly sliced

1/3 cup extra-virgin olive oil

1/2 cup dry white wine (leaning toward acidity, rather than mineral, dry quality)

1 pound fresh tomatoes, grated (I throw in skin, seeds, and all)

1/4 teaspoon dried oregano, or more

1/2 to 3/4 cup chicken broth

4 ounces Spanish cooking chorizo, cut up (see page 42)

2 tablespoons tomato paste, or as needed

1 Soak the salt cod in cold water for 2 days, changing the water a couple of times. Drain and rinse the fish. Remove and discard the bones and skin, and cut the cod into large bite-size pieces. Set aside.

2 Cook the potatoes in gently boiling salted water until just tender, for about 15 minutes. Drain and set aside. When cool enough to handle, slice thickly.

3 In a heavy saucepan or skillet, gently warm the sliced garlic in the olive oil until it turns lightly golden, add the wine, and cook for a minute or two, then stir in the tomatoes, oregano, and broth.

4 Cook over medium heat for 15 minutes or so, or long enough for the tomato mixture to thicken slightly and get flavorful.

5 Add the chorizo and tomato paste, stir together, and warm through, then add the cod and sliced potatoes. Do not stir into the sauce or you could break up the potatoes.

6 Heat through, tossing once or twice with a spatula; add a little extra hot water if the mixture seems too thick. Serve hot.

Variations

Spanish Cod and Potatoes, with the Abundance of the Sea

Add a handful of big fat prawns, or thin rings of squid, or a few crab legs, or all three, at the end of the cooking when you add the cod and sliced potatoes. Enjoy the saline fragrance they add to the pan.

Papas a las Flamencas

Instead of salt cod, add 1 teaspoon capers and 10 to 15 pimiento-stuffed green olives, cut into halves, at the last five minutes of cooking. This is good with or without the addition of shellfish.

Traditional Ligurian Gnocchi
with Fragrant Basil Pesto

○ ● ○ ◗ ○ ●

Some traditional things are difficult to improve on; after all, if you start with perfection—say, fragrant basil pesto—other spicy pastes may be very interesting and sprightly, but their main appeal is simply variety. The original paste based on fresh sweet basil and nuts, bound together with lashings of olive oil, pretty much cannot be beaten.

Ligurians, those dwellers of the Italian Riviera region that stretches from Nice, France, down through Genoa, Italy, and ends at the Tuscan border, love their pesto and eat it regularly, often several times a week. But they are very particular about what they eat it with; pasta cooked with potatoes and green beans is a favorite, also minestrone. My favorite, though, is gnocchi, the potato dumplings of the region that are sauced, and eaten, like pasta. I've even eaten plain ol' boiled potatoes and green beans dressed with pesto, without the pasta at all, and that is delish, if not authentic!

I've divided up the recipe into the potato gnocchi and the pesto. After all, you might want to serve it differently; say, splash the gnocchi with tomato sauce, or serve them with red wine–braised lamb and peas. I like to serve them with saucy Eastern European stews, such as paprikash and goulash, too. And one caveat for making gnocchi: you must use old—that is, from last year's crop—floury potatoes. Fresh potatoes make gummy gnocchi. They can't help themselves.

continued

continued

◇ Serves 4

3 large old baking potatoes (about 1 pound, 2 ounces), unpeeled and whole

2 teaspoons salt

2 tablespoons extra-virgin olive oil

1 egg, lightly beaten

1¼ to 1½ cups all-purpose flour, plus extra for rolling out

Butter, or olive oil, for the plate

Fragrant Basil Pesto (facing page)

1 Boil or bake the potatoes until they are very tender. If boiling, pour off the water and leave the potatoes to dry for a few minutes in the hot pot, covered, as you shake it back and forth for even drying. If baking, just remove from the oven and leave to cool slightly.

2 Peel when cool enough to handle; though all recipes for gnocchi say to do this while the potatoes are hot, I have had better luck waiting until later in the day when the potatoes are cool. The important thing is that the potato flesh is not gummy, but is light, dry, and fluffy.

3 Place the potato flesh in a bowl and mash or put through a ricer. Mix with half the salt, the olive oil, egg, and about two-thirds of the flour. Place the rest of the flour on a board and knead the potato dough (about 15 to 20 turns) into it, to absorb the flour. The dough should be slightly sticky but smooth and pliable.

4 Divide the dough into 4 or 5 segments; working with one segment at a time on a board, keeping the board floured, knead the segment of dough a few times, then roll out into a rope, about as thick as your forefinger or middle finger. Using a knife, cut the rope into 1½-inch pieces. Then with a fork, make little indentations on one side; the lumps will start to look like gnocchi now. Gently push them over to the floured side of the board or onto a baking sheet, and proceed until you have used all the potato dough.

5 Bring a big pot of water to a boil, add the remaining salt, and when the water is gently boiling, begin to add the gnocchi. You'll need to do this in batches; even a very big wide pot will still need about 2 or 3 batches. Do not overcrowd.

6 After a few minutes, the gnocchi will, one by one, come popping up to the surface. Remove with a slotted spoon or skimmer, and place on a buttered plate or baking dish. Repeat until all the gnocchi have been cooked.

7 Serve the gnocchi right away, with Fragrant Basil Pesto.

8 Gnocchi are fine to make up to 2 days ahead of time. Store in the refrigerator, and when ready to serve, reheat by putting them into boiling water to warm through and soften up. If you are serving them in a hot sauce instead of in fresh uncooked pesto, simply warm the cold gnocchi with the warm sauce.

Fragrant Basil Pesto

I'm giving a choice between the traditional Ligurian pine nuts, the more Tuscan walnuts,
or the Sicilian choice for pesto, almonds. All are delicious.

I like to use a food processor for this, and most Ligurians would agree—after proudly showing
off the huge, heirloom, generations-old mortar and pestle, they'll then show you what they really use:
the food processor. Still, you'll get a more fragrant and less harsh result by first pounding the
garlic in a mortar and pestle, and then tipping it into the food processor.

One more endearing quality of pesto: it freezes beautifully.

Serves 4

2 to 3 garlic cloves

**2 tablespoons pine nuts, or 15 to 20 walnuts, or blanched
skinned almonds**

1 bunch fresh basil

1/4 to 1/2 cup extra-virgin olive oil, or as desired

**3 to 4 ounces freshly grated Parmesan, Grana Padano,
pecorino, or half Parmesan and half pecorino**

Salt

1 Crush or cut up the garlic and add it to a food processor or
blender. Add the nuts and whirl into a fine meal, then add the
basil and whirl again. Add the olive oil, starting with about half
and working your way up until it forms a rich green sauce. Add
the cheese, and season to taste with salt, then whirl again.

2 To store in the refrigerator for up to a week, in a jar or bowl,
first submerge the pesto beneath a slick of olive oil, then cover
with a lid or plastic wrap.

Variations

Gnocchi con Vongole, Amalfi Coast Gnocchi with Clams and Tomatoes

**Toss boiled, drained gnocchi with a pan filled with sautéed clams
Campania-style (with tomatoes, oregano, and maybe a little slurp
of white wine).**

Gnocchi con Fagioli, Gnocchi with Fresh Beans

**Toss boiled, drained gnocchi with sautéed garlic and parsley;
cooked, drained fresh cranberry, borlotti, or other fresh beans;
and freshly grated Parmesan cheese to taste.**

Gnocchi with Pesto and Zucchini

Cook long strips of zucchini and toss with the gnocchi and pesto.

Yellow Curry of Potatoes and Chicken

○ ● ○ ◗ ○ ●

Richly fragrant, spicy and hot, Thai and Malaysian yellow curry paste is made from a palette
of spices and aromatics. Buy it from an Asian shop—a huge tub costs next to nothing—or make it yourself.
It's quite spicy, as in h-o-t, so you'll need to add it in small doses as you go along.
Don't worry, though, the coconut milk is soothing and balances out the heat, plus the potatoes
are bland, the lime sour, and the peanuts, well, nutty. It's a nice stew, sort of the best of East
and West, all rolled together into one cozy bowl.

◇ Serves 4

1½ to 2 tablespoons Yellow Curry Paste (facing page)

2 cups coconut milk

2 cups chicken broth

1 onion, chopped

1 pound small waxy potatoes (creamers), unpeeled

1 pound boneless chicken pieces, either white or dark meat, cut into bite-size chunks

3 to 4 limes, cut into quarters or wedges, or key limes cut in half, for squeezing

4 tablespoons chopped cilantro

3 to 4 tablespoons coarsely chopped toasted peanuts

1 Stir-fry the curry paste with half the coconut milk in a heavy skillet, *balti* pan, or wok; when it intensifies and thickens, add the broth and bring to a boil, then reduce the heat.

2 Add the onion and remaining coconut milk, cover, and continue cooking for about 30 minutes.

3 Add the potatoes, cover, and cook. When the potatoes are firm but almost tender, add the chicken, mixing in well, then cover, and simmer for a further 5 to 10 minutes for white meat, 10 to 15 minutes for dark meat.

4 Serve the curry in bowls; with a few chunks of meat, a handful of potatoes, a ladleful of curry, a wedge of lime, and a sprinkle of cilantro and peanuts.

Yellow Curry Paste

1 star anise

3 cardamom pods

3 cloves

One 1-inch piece cinnamon stick

1/2 teaspoon ground cinnamon

5 small hot red chiles, more if you desire or dare

1 medium-large onion, coarsely chopped

5 large garlic cloves, peeled

2 stalks lemongrass, trimmed down to its tender heart, cut into thin crosswise slices

One 1-inch piece fresh ginger, coarsely chopped

1/2 teaspoon ground cumin

1/4 to 1/2 teaspoon black peppercorns

5 macadamia nuts or peanuts, or 1 teaspoon peanut butter

1 tablespoon brown sugar

Salt

1 In a large, ungreased heavy skillet, lightly toast the star anise, cardamom, and cloves; cook them over medium-low heat for a few moments, shaking every so often, until they are toasted and smell fragrant. Remove from the heat and leave to cool.

2 Transfer the cooled spices to a food processor or coffee grinder, and whirl until they are coarsely ground. Add the cinnamon stick, ground cinnamon, chiles, onion, garlic, lemongrass, ginger, cumin, peppercorns, nuts, and brown sugar, and whirl until it's a chunky, smoothish paste. Season to taste with salt.

3 Store the excess in the freezer; I like to freeze it in small ice cube trays so that I can just pop out portions small enough to suit the size of the pan and the spicing required.

Variation
Yellow Curry of Potatoes and Seafood

I've been thinking that this curry might be very tasty with prawns or other shellfish—allow about 5 minutes cooking time once you add the shellfish to the pot.

Savory, Spicy
Middle Eastern Pot
of Tomatoey Potatoes and Meat

○ ● ○ ◉ ○ ●

Deliciously homey, as well as spicy and fragrant—this Middle Eastern braise is easy to make for one or two, or for a whole tent full. Double or triple, as you like. Stewing beef or lamb, instead of the ground beef? Go right ahead. The flavor is all about the meaty zesty gravy being absorbed by the potatoes. And if you're a vegetarian: the dish is delicious using chickpeas instead of meat.

A bowl of yogurt, some good flatbread or sourdough bread, and a salad of crunchy raw vegetables make this a meal; regardless of the accompaniments, I like eating this stew from a bowl, letting the savory perfumes rise and tickle my nose, making everything even more delicious.

◇ Serves 4 as a small plate, 2 as a main dish

2 tablespoons extra-virgin olive oil

1 onion, chopped

8 ounces ground beef

4 medium-large waxy potatoes, preferably white or yellow-skinned

5 garlic cloves, thinly sliced

1/2 large flavorful green bell pepper, sliced into strips

One 14 1/2-ounce can tomatoes, including the juices, or 2 1/2 pounds ripe fresh tomatoes, diced

1 teaspoon paprika

1/2 teaspoon cumin

1/4 teaspoon turmeric

Seeds from 3 to 5 cardamom pods (depending on how large and how fragrant they are)

A pinch or two of allspice

A small pinch of red pepper flakes, or a gentle shake of cayenne (or use a slightly, only slightly, spicy chile pepper, such as poblano)

Water to barely cover (or half water, half broth)

1 teaspoon bouillon powder, or 1/2 to 1 bouillon cube (if not using broth)

3 tablespoons chopped cilantro (include root and stems, for added flavor)

Salt and pepper

1 In a heavy skillet, heat half the olive oil over medium-high heat and lightly sauté the onion until just softened, then add the beef, and break it up into little chunks, cooking together until the meat is lightly browned in places but not cooked through. Do not let the onion brown too much, just a touch of gold. Remove to a bowl and set aside while you cook the potatoes.

2 Add the rest of the olive oil to the pan, then add the potatoes, and lightly cook in the oil, which has some flavor from the onion and the meat. Cook for 5 minutes or so on each side, then return the meat and onion to the pan, add the garlic, bell pepper, tomatoes, paprika, cumin, turmeric, cardamom seeds, allspice, red pepper flakes, water to cover, and bouillon powder or cube, if using.

3 Bring heat up to medium, and cook for about 20 minutes, turning once or twice. Do not stir, or keep turning, as you want the potatoes to stay as whole as possible and not break up. You could also bake this in the oven instead of cooking it on the stove top.

4 For the last 5 or 10 minutes, raise the heat to high and cook until the liquid boils down to a thick, flavorful sauce. Do not let it get too dry, nor should it be too soupy. You want it very flavorful, and nicely saucy, stewy, and somewhat soupy.

5 Sprinkle in the cilantro, and toss to mix it through. Season to taste with salt and pepper, and serve hot, in bowls.

Variations
Turkish Bowl of Homey Meat and Potatoes
Ferah Tanadar, a fellow food-lover from Ankara, Turkey, and an advisor for the Turkish Pistachio Board, shared with me her family's bowl of comfy, savory meat and potatoes. Follow the recipe as directed, but omit the turmeric, cardamom, and cilantro. Simmer on top of the stove, or bake in the oven; when it's ready, put your feet up, relax, and enjoy.

Eritrean Potatoes
Omit the meat and cilantro. Halve the amount of tomatoes, and use a hefty amount of Berbere, the Eritrean/Ethiopian hot chile pepper, instead of hot pepper flakes, to taste, as hot as you dare.

Greek Veal, Pork, or Turkey
Stuffed with Feta and Braised with Wine and Potatoes

○ ● ○ ● ○ ●

This is inspired by similar dishes I've eaten on the Greek island of Zákinthos. Stuffing the roast with feta not only salts your roast from the inside but gives added nuances of flavor, too, while the chopped red bell pepper gives vegetal freshness. And the potatoes . . . ah . . . the potatoes absorb all the delicious flavors of the juices.

◇ Serves 4 to 6

2 small to medium boneless turkey thighs, or a 3-pound boneless leg of veal or pork, butterflied

1 red bell pepper, chopped

4 ounces feta cheese

3 garlic cloves, chopped

1 onion, chopped

3 tablespoons extra-virgin olive oil

1/2 cup dry white wine

1 cup chicken broth

1 1/2 teaspoons fresh thyme, chopped, or 1/2 teaspoon dried

Salt and black pepper

6 medium-size all-purpose potatoes, neither floury nor waxy, peeled and cut into quarters or halves

Juice of 1/2 lemon

1 Preheat the oven to 350°F. Lay the roast out and pat flat, inside facing up. Sprinkle with the bell pepper, feta cheese, garlic, and onion, then roll back up and tie with string.

2 Place in a roasting pan and drizzle the roast with the olive oil, then pour the wine and broth into the pan. Sprinkle the roast with thyme and black pepper to taste. The feta is salty, so add salt only if needed. Cover with foil for 45 minutes to 1 hour.

3 Bake at 350°F until the meat is half cooked. Remove and discard the foil, then add the potatoes to the pan, and a little water if needed to keep a liquid depth of about 2 inches, then return to the oven and continue to bake for a further 40 minutes or so, or until the meat is tender and cooked through, the potatoes are tender but not mushy, and the liquid is a flavorful sauce.

4 Squeeze the lemon over the top, remove the meat to a platter, keep warm, and let sit for 10 minutes. If the pan juices are watery, pour into a saucepan and boil to reduce to an intense jus.

5 Slice and serve, the meat surrounded by the potatoes, with the pan juices spooned over the top.

Malaysian Stew
of Black Mushrooms, Tofu, Miso, and Potatoes

○ ● ○ ● ○ ●

The glorious combination of cuisines and cultures that makes up Malaysia is most apparent in its pots, pans, and bowls. For instance, this dish: savory and Asian, a compilation of everything that screams out Far East flavors—black mushrooms, tofu, miso, soy sauce, ginger . . . and . . . potatoes? Oh, the Malaysians love potatoes, and serve them in nearly every coconutty curried, spice-redolent stew. This dish, if I am being truthful, is a telescoping of two different *nonya* dishes: a simmer of chicken with black mushrooms, miso, and potatoes, and a stir-fry of simmered vegetables and tofu.

If you want to be authentic, use dark-meat chicken in place of tofu; if you like meatballs—and I happen to be an aficionado, big time—add those instead. Whichever meat or tofu you add to the pot, be sure the potatoes are small and flavorful. The potatoes in Malaysia are dense, with a wonderful, nutty flavor; some have an ordinary darkish brown skin, others have a thicker black one. Delicious on their own, roasted on an open fire, Malaysian potatoes are also delicious tossed into nearly anything savory you have stewing on your stove.

◇ Serves 4, in a meal with other dishes, or 2 as a main plate

2½ to 3 ounces dried black or shiitake mushrooms

Oil for frying

8 ounces firm tofu, cut into bite-size pieces and patted dry with a paper towel

3 garlic cloves, coarsely chopped

3 green onions, thinly sliced

One ½-inch piece ginger, chopped

2 tablespoons sweet sherry

1 to 2 tablespoons dark soy sauce

½ to 1 teaspoon rice vinegar, plus a drop or two extra if needed

2 tablespoons sugar

1 cup vegetable or chicken broth

1½ tablespoons miso (1 year old), or Chinese fermented bean sauce

8 ounces small new potatoes, cut into halves or bite-size pieces, unpeeled

1 Place the mushrooms in a bowl and cover with boiling water. Leave, covered, to sit and soften, for at least 30 minutes. Remove from the soaking water, and save the water to use for your sauce.

2 Fill a medium nonstick skillet with 1/4 inch oil and heat over medium-high heat. Fry the tofu until golden browned on the bottom, then turn over and brown the second side. Remove from the skillet and drain on a paper towel.

3 In a skillet, wok, or heavy large saucepan, stir-fry the garlic, green onions, and ginger in a tablespoon of oil until fragrant, for a minute or two. Add the softened mushrooms.

4 Add the sherry, 1 tablespoon of the soy sauce, the vinegar, sugar, and chicken broth, and cook for about 5 minutes or so, then pour the mushroom-soaking liquid in, keeping the last tablespoon or two from being added as it has all the bits and impurities. Discard that last spoonful.

5 Add 1 tablespoon of the miso, along with the potatoes, then cover and cook for about 15 minutes, or until the potatoes are soft. Add the reserved tofu and cook together for about 5 minutes.

6 Stir in the remaining miso, and taste for seasoning; add the remaining soy sauce only if needed, as well as a drop or two extra rice vinegar.

Patata Pitta

Crisp Filo Pies of Mashed Potato, Cheese, and Olive Paste

○ ● ○ ● ○ ●

Flaky pastries surrounding herbed mashed potatoes—there was a shop that made these right across the street from our hotel in Athens, so I bought a selection of *pittas* for our flight home, so nicely wrapped in paper, the little wrapping secured with a rubber band, a handful of napkins alongside for tidy eating.

These *patata pittas* are like über-delicious potato knishes, the Eastern European Jewish pastries that are stuffed with potatoes mashed with onion.

◇ Serves 4

2 baking potatoes (about 12 ounces), such as russets, unpeeled

Salt

3 ounces feta cheese, crumbled

3 ounces mild white cheese, such as *kasseri*, Provolone, mild Asiago, or Jack

1 heaping tablespoon sour cream, or Greek yogurt

1/2 to 1 teaspoon fresh marjoram leaves, coarsely chopped

1 shallot, chopped

1 egg

Black pepper

Flour for the board

8 ounces prepared puff pastry

4 tablespoons black olive paste, or as needed

1 Cut the potatoes into about three big chunks per potato, place in a saucepan with salted water to cover, and bring to a boil. Reduce the heat to medium and cook until the potatoes are just tender; pour the water out, and when cool enough to handle, peel off the skins.

2 Preheat the oven to 400°F. Mash the potatoes with a fork or potato masher, then mix in the feta, white cheese, sour cream, marjoram, shallot, and egg. Mix well and taste for pepper and additional seasoning. You probably won't need salt, as feta is salty, as is the olive paste you will spread on the pastry.

3 On a lightly floured board, roll the puff pastry to about 1/8 inch thick, then lay it out on a nonstick baking sheet.

4 Spread the black olive paste over the pastry, then spoon the potato filling into the center. Fold the edges over, making a sort of oblong galette, that is, a flat pielike pastry with an inside strip of potato exposed.

5 Bake for about 20 minutes or until golden and crisp. Serve hot.

Index

Index

Index

Table of Equivalents

The exact equivalents in the following tables have been rounded for convenience.

Liquid/Dry Measures

U.S.	Metric
¼ teaspoon	1.25 milliliters
½ teaspoon	2.5 milliliters
1 teaspoon	5 milliliters
1 tablespoon (3 teaspoons)	15 milliliters
1 fluid ounce (2 tablespoons)	30 milliliters
¼ cup	60 milliliters
⅓ cup	80 milliliters
½ cup	120 milliliters
1 cup	240 milliliters
1 pint (2 cups)	480 milliliters
1 quart (4 cups, 32 ounces)	960 milliliters
1 gallon (4 quarts)	3.84 liters
1 ounce (by weight)	28 grams
1 pound	454 grams
2.2 pounds	1 kilogram

Lengths

U.S.	Metric
⅛ inch	3 millimeters
¼ inch	6 millimeters
½ inch	12 millimeters
1 inch	2.5 centimeters

Oven Temperatures

Fahrenheit	Celsius	Gas
250	120	½
275	140	1
300	150	2
325	160	3
350	180	4
375	190	5
400	200	6
425	220	7
450	230	8
475	240	9
500	260	10